INFORMATION WAR

INFORMATION WAR

AMERICAN PROPAGANDA, FREE SPEECH
AND OPINION CONTROL SINCE 9/11

NANCY SNOW

FOREWORD BY GREG PALAST

01056

An Open Me book

SEVEN STORIES ESS / NEW YORK

In Canada: Hushion House, 36 Northline Road, Toronto, Ontario M4B 3E2

In the U.K.: Turnaround Publisher Services Ltd., Unit 3, Olympia Trading Estate, Coburg Road, Wood Green, London N22 6TZ

In Australia: Palgrave Macmillan, 627 Chapel Street, South Yarra, VIC 3141

Cover design: Greg Ruggiero
Cover image derived from a 1943 U.S. Civil Service Commission propaganda poster.

ISBN 1-58322-557-9

Printed in Canada.

9 8 7 6 5 4 3 2 1

I'D LIKE TO DEDICATE THIS BOOK to the following students: Aaron, Andrew, Brooke, Calvin, Gary, Jay, Jed, Jenifer, Karen, Kimberly, Lauren, Lindsay, Mark, Natasha, and Rebecca, in my spring 2002 "Propaganda, Terrorism and Media" course at the Annenberg School for Communication, University of Southern California. After 9/11, I chose to rededicate myself to university teaching and working more closely with communication and journalism students. It was the students' dedication to the information-war topic that kept me motivated to write, even as global events continued to shock and discourage. My love for teaching and learning is directly related to the spirit and dedication of these university students and those I hope to teach. The truth is, they really teach me a lot about life and hope. In the spirit of mutual understanding and learning, I present this collection of writings on the *Information War*.

> *Be patient toward all that is unsolved in your heart and try to love the questions themselves.*
> —RAINER MARIE RILKE, from *Letters to a Young Poet*

Contents

□ □ □

Foreword

BY GREG PALAST

□ □ □

DICTATORSHIPS PERSUADE with truncheons and dungeons. Propaganda, Noam Chomsky tells us, is the mark of a *democracy*, necessary when those more direct means are unavailable. By that measure, the United States may be the most democratic among nations—with few political prisoners, but home to the largest, longest, deepest river of burbling B.S. known to man—home of the brave and of double talk, nonsense, half-truths, Tom Brokaw, disinformation, baloney, CNN, white lies, black lies, and Katie Couric. "And here, the President is waving to us from his helicopter!"

When all I want is some truth. Problem is, we need a decoder ring to sort the truth from the trash. And that's what this book is, your translation manual, your instructions for deconstructing the machinery of mendacity.

Professor Snow is our Toto...like Dorothy's little dog in *The Wizard of Oz*, she goes behind the curtain to expose the awful little man projecting that big fake image on the giant screen. Snow rips back the curtain on the agencies, programs and methods of our nation's official propagandists, both the ones you've heard of, like the USIA, and the ones you haven't, like the "Office of Strategic Influence." If the name of that little pustule on our government's organizational chart doesn't give you the willies, Snow's portrait of it and the propaganda czar, Undersecretary of State for Public Diplomacy Charlotte Beers, certainly will. Ms. Beers, whom George W. Bush put in charge of convincing the world's religion-and-resentment-stuffed billions *NOT TO KILL US*, came to her post fresh from running ad campaigns for Uncle Ben's Rice. Lord help us.

It's just such combinations of pinheaded arrogance and boobery that characterizes the Bush administration's intellectual weaponry for the War on Terror. That's what Snow tells us in horrifying detail; and as a former apparatchik in America's ministry of propaganda, the USIA, she can speak from her experience in the belly of the clown.

A couple of years ago, a mischievous U.S. State Department consul convinced USAID to send me to Brazil. I followed, city to city, in the footsteps of Mack McLarty, Henry Kissinger's business partner, formerly Bill Clinton's chief of staff. McLarty was prancing about, trying to sell Brazil on the wonders of selling off their water and power systems (preferably cheaply, to his clients). Weirdly, the United States government paid me a packet to explain that, in America, we tend to run such snakeoil salesmen out of town. McLarty failed to mention that, in the United States, privatization and deregulation are on the run. I explained that almost all water systems are publicly owned in America, the result of a huge public uprising (the Populist movement), ninety years ago, against the water and power barons. It surprised my audiences to learn that well-organized anti-corporate mass movements have made the United States the only nation outside of Canada and Guyana with open forums (public-service commissions, the nuclear regulatory commission, and more) which democratically control the investments and even the prices of private corporations.

This story of America the Democratic was a winning advertisement for our nation—but one that conflicted with the mission of our official propagandists: to justify the projection of United States military and commercial power, to put gloves on the claws of Kissinger-McLarty Associates. What the Bushmen of Washington *DON'T* want is the propagation of seditious ideas—freedom of speech, of press, of religion, freedom from want—that America's best propagandists (Tom Paine, Thomas Jefferson, Franklin Roosevelt) deployed to inspire the planet.

Now, instead of Rushmore-worthy giants like Jefferson, we have the sales force from Lilliput: America's world image is left to Uncle Ben's jingle writer who announced that the "brand" she is selling is George W. Bush.

I'm not laughing. These people are SCARY. Think about it: our minister of propaganda is supposed to be explaining to the Arab street why American citizens shouldn't be sliced, diced, and bombed; and what does Ms. Beers dangle in front of their faces? A smirking rich white kid, Brand "W"—which flopped even in the USA (after all, Americans voted against that guy by a substantial margin). And if the wretched of the earth don't warm to Dubya, we beam them images of war profiteer Dick Cheney skulking in his hideaway, Shoot 'em First Don "Mad Dog" Rumsfeld, the offensive secretary of defense, and John Poindexter who was convicted of aiding terrorists in the 1980s, appointed to head up Bush's office of "Total Information Awareness," which has since been shut down in response to public outrage. Even Henry the K was unlocked from his political crypt by our president to join the team. Our plea to the world is spoken by armed and dangerous refugees from corporate boards shrieking, "You're with us or you're against us."

I'm afraid. And after you read all the dirty details in this book, you may be too.

—Greg Palast, New York and London

Truth and Consequences

If those in charge of our society—politicians, corporate executives, and owners of press and television—can dominate our ideas, they will be secure in their power. They will not need soldiers patrolling the streets. We will control ourselves.

—HOWARD ZINN

▢ ▢ ▢

GROWING UP IN THE UNITED STATES, I was taught that the most beautiful word in the American lexicon was freedom. "My country 'tis of thee, sweet land of liberty." Although my citizenship was an accident of birth, I felt part of a chosen lucky few who were born into the greatest country in the world. I was also taught that, unlike the citizens of Communist countries who were born under a dark cloud of tyranny and ruthless dictators, we were a free people, blessed by God with an abundance of government-protected liberties—free press, free speech, free expression. In grade school, I pledged allegiance to these freedoms and genuflected to a set of sacred documents known as the United States Constitution, the Declaration of Independence and the Bill of Rights. To me, the First Amendment read like a favorite Psalm:

> Congress shall make no law respecting an establishment of religion, or prohibiting the free exercise thereof; or abridging the freedom of speech, or of the press; or the right of the people peaceably to assem-

ble, and to petition the Government for a redress of grievances.

I thought that "We the people," the first three words in the Preamble to the United States Constitution said it all about what it means to live in a democracy, an open society, where government represents the public good and certain rights of its citizens—life, liberty, and the pursuit of happiness as well as equality. If our government failed in that promise, then "it is the right of the people to alter or to abolish it, and to institute a new government."

Unlike those poor souls who lived in a one-party state, we Americans had two parties, Democratic and Republican. Instead of just one central power, we had three—the executive (the presidency), the legislative (Congress), and the judicial (Supreme Court)—that would keep their eyes on one another so that power would be balanced and corruption checked. The numbers game favored the free over the unfree. On top of it all, I had a choice among dozens of kinds of chewing gum. If I complained, it took about two seconds for someone to say, "Look at the alternative." A or B. Free or Unfree.

As I grew up in the land of the free, I began to see that freedom did not mean a full range of choices but was narrowly defined as what was generally acceptable within a dominant framework. There were prudent ways of defining democracy and freedom, and there were imprudent ways. Democracy turned out to be what was exercised through indirect and very proper channels. A free press turned out to be free to those who could own one. The dominant press, radio, and television were called the mass media as an insiders' joke, but I never saw my neighbor or teacher on my TV set. The masses had the "mass" media but we weren't expected to have the brainpower to make the tough policy decisions, such as where

13

or how "our" government was going to interfere in other people's lives. It just did. Something to do with protecting our freedom abroad and making the world safe for democracy. Walter Lippmann, the treasure of American journalism, called us a phantom public. He wrote, "The public must be put in its place...so that each of us can live free of the trampling and the roar of a bewildered herd." Instead of ordinary folks, I did see a lot of people in the mass media with very impressive credentials who were introduced as experts, analysts, or pundits. They seemed to know better or to have information that we didn't have, which led them to some very smart conclusions. They often made us feel afraid, as if the world were a scary place, with a lot of people who were out to take away our freedoms. This feeling made us rely even more on their expertise so that we could feel safer, more secure.

Since I'm a teacher, I like to tell my students to think outside the box of what's acceptable or prudent or talked about in polite circles. I'd like to tell them that the decision-makers and experts don't know as well as do citizens and ordinary people how to represent "our" own interests. It's probably unwise and not a good career decision to suggest that they think outside their comfort zones of acceptable thought. After all, I keep hearing in my head, "Look at all you have. Then look at the alternative. Freedom or terror."

This book is a tribute to liberating alternatives to the present order of things. It takes a look at the chief American propagandists such as Bill Bennett, George W. Bush, and Donald Rumsfeld, who triumph order over expression and those patriotic dissenters Barbara Lee and Janis Heaphy, two courageous critics of the present order of things, whose dedication to intellectual criticism and the public good should be cloned. I attempt to analyze, albeit briefly, some of the propaganda conditions in our recent American history that gave rise to the present order, which may explain in part why America remains such a deeply anti-intellectual society as a whole. I reveal how George Bush and his brain Karl Rove have borrowed heavily from the wartime president Harry Truman and the World War I propagandist George Creel to map out American's militaristic destiny (and current war on terrorism) destiny as one entwined with Truth, Freedom, and Democracy. There's really no smoking gun, but a public library to reveal the mass manipulation of language and thought control under which we operate as a nation. So where do we turn for straight talk and clear thinking? The historical role of the American press to act as watchdog against corruption and abuse was relegated to history and journalism textbooks when in June 2003, a three-person Republican majority on the Federal Communications Commission headed by our nation's chief foreign policy advisor's son, decided that the likes of Time Warner, Clear Channel, and News Corporation needed *less* public regulation and oversight and more concentration and control over our every waking minute. So if it's not the responsibility of the American press to tell the truth (and run?), how about the American school, college, or university? As I show in efforts by such post-9/11 pop-up organizations as Americans for Victory Over Terrorism (AVOT) and the American Council of Trustees and Alumni (ACTA), American campuses have been scapegoated as harbingers of all that's wrong with America's youth. My country, right or wrong—not my country, right and wrong.

So where I can we turn for solace? To our modern Tom Paines like Howard Zinn, Noam Chomsky, Michael Moore, Tim Robbins, Susan Sarandon, and others who know better than to only speak when spoken to. They speak because it's their duty to represent the truly American patriotic legacy of questioning our government, even when it's not fashionable or time-sensitive (pre- and post-war) to do so. They share good company with Representative Barbara Lee of California—all have been marked as traitors to the United States of America.

But this is no time to let a little name-calling spoil one's day.

Picture a Friday evening in April 2002. The sun is setting in Newport Beach (think Beverly Hills with waves and lots of enhancement and augmentation surgeons). The Travel Channel named Newport Beach one of America's best beaches in 2002 and "Best Classic California Beach," where the "Endless Summer" of the Beach Boys comes to mind (slow, mellow, and hanging ten). Newport Beach is not what comes to mind when you think of the U.S. war on terrorism or war in general. Nevertheless, I arrive at the Newport Beach Public Library to hear another classic tune from one of those questionable American patriots. Howard Zinn is addressing a mix of library benefactors, former students who have found the American dream behind the Orange Curtain (Orange County), and the curious who seem to marvel at the live display of a radical American historian. There are some, like me, who come because Howard Zinn is our intellectual rock star. He's a real beautiful mind, author of the seminal work *A People's History of the United States*, and outspoken advocate for non-violence and social justice. I'm there hanging ten with the other dissident upstarts.

Being in the presence of this octogenarian almost brings on tears of joy. Living in a culture in which we struggle to free ourselves from endless corporate jingles that loop in our head from Britney Spears to the latest Miller Lite ad, I enjoy a rare opportunity to hear someone who's so damned authentic. You couldn't manufacture this guy or his history. He was born into a working-class family, were his parents had grade school educations while their son completed his Ph.D. in history at Columbia University. From the slums of Brooklyn, he became a shipyard worker during his college-age years. He volunteered for the Army Air Corps and served as a bombardier in World War II, service that gave him access to the GI Bill that financed his higher education. His war experience, the one that produced the Greatest Generation, shaped his anti-war sentiment. From 35,000 feet, you can't hear screams or see blood. From that experience he understood how easy it is for atrocities to be committed in modern warfare——from a distance. He tells us about his final air mission. Everyone knew that the war was about to end in a matter of weeks. At one o'clock in the morning, he was awakened and told that his squadron was going to bomb a little French town near Bordeaux called Royan. Nobody asked why. They did what they were told. "You don't ask questions at war briefings," he says. A couple of thousand German soldiers were holed up in the town, waiting for the war to end. But this time he would carry a different type of bomb, not the usual demolition bomb but canisters filled with jellied gasoline. It was napalm. The entire town was destroyed—the Germans, and the French who were still there.

A library trustee who had earlier introduced herself as working "with the same firm as Ted Olsen," introduces Professor Zinn as "a person whose progressive views are rarely heard in Orange County." Maybe so. But you could also add the United States and the world. In the days following 9/11, Howard Zinn published an anti-war essay, "Violence Doesn't Work," in which he condemned the old way of thinking that dominates our headlines. He wrote,

> We need to decide that we will not go to war, whatever the reason is conjured up by the politicians or the media, because war in our time is always indiscriminate, a war against innocents, a war against children. War is terrorism, magnified a hundred times.[1]

It's April 19, 2002, and Howard Zinn is reminding me why I can't be neutral on this moving war train. It has a lot to do with opinion control and propaganda slogans. The warriors and those who profit from war try to persuade us that we're one big happy family. It's always "our" national interest, national security, national defense, instead of "somebody's" security and interest. These "united we stand, divided we fall" categories obscure real class differences, the rich and the poor, and all those nervous people in between. Does war solve fundamental problems? Zinn replies, "What happens in war is that everyone gets corrupted." In the meantime, we're lulled into a false sense of security where Exxon Mobil and the President speak as if their interests are the collective interest of everyone from Watts to Boston's Back Bay.

Howard Zinn asks the Newport Beach library audience to consider something about the war on terrorism. Maybe, just maybe, we didn't go to war in Afghanistan to fight terrorism. Maybe it was an action to stop us from truly thinking about what to do about terrorism. We had to do something, but as Zinn tells us, the strange logic of war is that when nations don't know what to do, they often go to war or declare war (war on drugs, war on terrorism.) The inverse connection is the evidence, from Northern Ireland to Israel, that going to war actually increases terrorism.

The following day I catch the Z train at Newport Harbor High, where a hundred high school kids arrive at high noon on a Saturday, some with their dog-eared copies of Zinn's *A People's History* in tow. This time, it's an open forum, where the kids can ask anything. And they do. One student asks, "Is it true that you don't like the United States?" To this, he replies, "I like the people; it's the government I'm not too sure of." He tells these young minds to be skeptical of what their leaders tell them. It's clear how much he loves the people of the United States.

> The Declaration of Independence says that governments are artificial creations set up by the people to accomplish certain ends. When governments become destructive toward these ends, it's the right of the people to alter or abolish the government. If we have the right to abolish the government, then we have the right to criticize it. In that case, it's the government being unpatriotic.[2]

Howard Zinn's antidote to the corrupting influence of government and corporate power is not the lobby or the boardroom. It's the American street. People must not take this country for granted. They've got to organize, join movements, and become activists. "The ultimate solution is not with the people on top, " says Zinn. "The ultimate solution is for people in the streets to create an atmosphere for people on top to be accountable."

It is then that I realize that Howard Zinn doesn't really have to be flying across the country from Boston. He's reached the age of retirement as a professor emeritus from Boston University. He's here because he cannot stay neutral on this peace and social justice movement train. He tells the students about an anti-war poster he saw during the 1960s: *War is good for business. Invest your son.* That slogan revealed a discrepancy between what we're supposed to be fighting for—peace, liberty, freedom—and what we're really fighting for—somebody's interests. Granfalloons. The Z train has its own slogan: *Democracy is good for people. Invest yourself.* Now that's some truth-telling.

In the spirit of Professor Zinn, I hope this book reveals some truth and will motivate a little street-taking protest and lots of organizing.

Bermuda Mind Triangle

PROPAGANDA, TERRORISM, AND MEDIA

☐ ☐ ☐

JUST THREE DAYS BEFORE the first military attacks in Afghanistan, the London-based magazine *The Economist* published an article that openly acknowledged an American war that was already under way and laying the groundwork for the shooting war: the propaganda war. "That word has come to have a derogatory meaning, of the dissemination of untruths. In this case, America's task is (in truth) to disseminate truths, about its motives, about its intentions, about its current and past actions in Israel and Iraq, about its views of Islam. For all that, however, this part of the war promises to be no easier to win than the many other elements of the effort."[3] It is that article, along with my previous book, *Propaganda Inc.*, about United States propaganda, that prompted this collection of writings about America's information and propaganda war, which is well under way in the post–September 11 world. The *Economist* stated quite accurately that the propaganda war "is needed to sustain the immediate battle but also to win the peace." Where I part company is with the way the United States government is going about its approach to winning the peace.

Propaganda campaigns generally seed the soil for success-ful military operations and are often used to make a person conform to one line of thinking about a military operation or, in this case, a war on terrorism. We do not generally view propaganda as a euphemism for critical thinking; in fact, propaganda, as viewed in the context of mass persuasion that benefits the manufacturer and sender, often begins where critical thinking ends. This is why as a propaganda scholar and communications professor in the United States, I wanted to provide a brief critical portrait of America's information war. This book is neither comprehensive nor objective; it is written in the spirit of service and caution, perhaps even a warning shot across our bow.

Jacques Ellul, author of the classic text *Propaganda*, wrote that "to warn a political system of the menace hanging over it does not imply an attack on it, but it is the greatest service one can render the system."[4] Forty years ago, Ellul wrote in the book's preface that "in the world today, there are three great propaganda blocs: the U.S.S.R., China, and the United States." Were one to continue his analysis, today there are only two.

As luck would have it, in March 2002 I was able to interview Konrad Kellen, the translator of Ellul's book from French into English and author of the introduction to the American edition of *Propaganda*. Kellen, a former RAND scholar who is now in his eighties and living in Los Angeles, reminded me that Ellul's greatest contribution to the literature on propaganda was his proposition that propaganda is most effective when it is least noticeable. What the American people don't know, he said, is that "American propaganda here is more hidden." In a controlled society, propaganda is obvious and reluctantly tolerated for fear of the negative consequences. In an open society, such as the United States, the hidden and integrated nature of the propaganda best convinces people that they are not being manipulated. This is why the concept of propaganda in the United States is so problematic and painted in a strictly negative light. Propaganda is supposed to be something that Hitler mastered and that his filmmaker Leni Riefenstahl made into a perverse art form. It is not supposed to be part of an open society. But indeed, as I learned from my conversation with Kellen, what is even more propagandistic is the United States President's message among us that Americans are do-gooders in a global battle against evil. Kellen said that President Bush, for all his post-9/11 popularity, has "mastered the art of saying nothing" and that it's these "platitudes of emptiness" that reinforce mistaken ideas, propaganda notions, about how to fight a war that may have no end—the war on terrorism. The propaganda war is the most integrated part of the new war on terror; it's the part that is most hidden from view but also the most pervasive.

Most people want to be smart about everything and have a need to inform themselves, but what happens is that we get a lot of commercialized information in the service of profit-making, misinformation, and ignorance. It is controlled information, not designed for community empowerment or popular education that aims to further the ability of people to think for themselves.[5] The world is not divided into distinct categories of white hats and black hats, do-gooders and evildoers, unless you want to believe the world that Spider-Man inhabits. American propaganda is the sugar pill that makes the bitter truth go down. To paraphrase Spider-Man, "It is our gift. It is our curse."

"Un-American" is a favorite name-calling device to stain the reputation of someone who disagrees with official policies and positions. It conjures up old red-baiting techniques that stifle free speech and dissent on public issues. It creates a chilling effect on people to stop testing the waters of our democratic right to question the motives of our government. Since September 11, 2001, we've become deluged with name-calling devices. This is why Representative Barbara Lee (D-

CA) was referred to as the lone dissenter in Congress and called a traitor by some such as the talk-show host Rush Limbaugh, when she very judiciously could not issue a blank check to the administration to carry out the war on terrorism however it seemed fit, forty-eight hours after September 11. She was honoring the United States Constitution and its system of checks and balances in the face of the freewheeling whims of an executive run amuck. She should have been applauded and heralded for her conservative and cautious approach to the use of power and force in response to the 9/11 attacks, but instead she was called a traitor and un-American.

The new propaganda methods in the war on terror include language manipulation and traditional marketing techniques to "sell" America to the world. These include a $520 million Congressional appropriation to focus on so-called disaffected populations in the Middle East and South Asia and the establishment of a twenty-four hour Arabic-language satellite news network called Radio Sawa (meaning "together"), along with a proposed Middle East Television Network to compete with Al Jazeera, the Qatar-based CNN of the Arab-speaking world. Before she resigned her position for health reasons in March 2003, Undersecretary of State for Public Diplomacy Charlotte Beers, whom I examine at length later in the book, undertook the biggest public-relations effort in the history of United States foreign policy, using traditional public-relations and marketing techniques like focus groups, market research, and video projects about Muslim Americans to show the United States to the world as a tolerant and open society. Beers announced that she would use one of the "best practices" of modern advertising—a strong emphasis on the emotional with the rational; but from what we know about modern American advertising techniques, the emotional always wins out. As the contemptible but clever German Nazi propagandist Joseph Goebbels pointed out, "There is no need for propaganda to be rich in intellectual content." Instead, the emphasis remains one of empty omnibus words and phrases like freedom and democracy, which have no set meaning but can strike responsive emotional chords. "The propagandist," wrote Alfred McClung Lee in *How to Understand Propaganda*, "thus strives for simplicity and vividness coupled with speed and broad impact. He stimulates popular emotional drives in existing grooves which are most likely to forward his objectives. In so doing, he must for the most part bypass factual discussion and debate of an adequate sort."[6] Read on and you'll see how such tactics were utilized with limited success by Charlotte Beers.

What's so fascinating about all these propaganda efforts in the War on Terror is how reconstituted they appear. The United States has a one-hundred-year history of marrying commerce with politics and tapping public relations to "brand" America abroad. President Woodrow Wilson told the International Congress of Salesmanship to "go out and sell goods that will make the world more comfortable and more happy and convert them to the principles of America." That was in 1916. Is today all that much different? No, not really, but it's more intensified now because we have the technology age to aid the efforts to brand the product America, and we have the unpredictable dark cloud of that catch-all new enemy, terrorism, magnifying our efforts.

Charlotte Beers at one time headed J. Walter Thompson, one of the top ten advertising firms in the world. George Creel, the head of the American Committee on Public Information (CPI) in World War I, called on CEO James Webb Young of J. Walter Thompson, who led information war efforts to demoralize the German people. Victoria de Grazia of the *New York Times* describes how United States propaganda efforts, merging with democratic capitalist ideals, functioned throughout the last century: "Publicity, with private sector support, was the handmaiden of a government that presented itself as opposed to heavy-handed involvement abroad and sought to circumvent autocratic leaders to get the humane, rational message of the American people directly to peoples with similar aspirations. Other regimes may propagate hard-nosed ideology, but American democracy had lofty ideals."[7] There is no other country in the world that matches ours for developing such close links between commerce (salesmanship) and the business of government (statesmanship). None. Since World War I, advertising has mixed with selling war, foreign aid, and even cultural exchanges.

This situation creates a real dilemma for the United States government in the twenty-first century as it engages in a global war on terrorism. How can the world's undisputed superpower avoid overplaying its hand by mixing the Big Sell with a government effort to persuade people elsewhere that American society is tolerant and desirable? It cannot. We will continue to read occasional reports from the Council on Foreign Relations or the U.S. Public Diplomacy Advisory Commission, their members gnashing their teeth over our hyperadvertising approach to reshaping America's image in the world. This is what the United States is to the world—the ultimate salesman. We are, like it or not, the world's Barnum & Bailey. We shouldn't be too surprised therefore that anti-Americanism is in fact on a steep rise after the United States had global sympathy following 9/11. The Bush administration's go-it-alone militarism has fanned the flames of this growing enmity.

The Bush administration's propaganda efforts on Iraq underscored the administrations new doctrine of militant unilateralism—that the United States needs the world more as its audience than as its partner. Until and unless the world sees a picture of American society filled with debate and dissent about the direction our country is taking, we shouldn't hold out great hope for any short-term gains in improving our global image, whether or not the government cools it on the advertising. What we can do is reach out with friends here and abroad to mount open dissent and protest against a United States administration that is neither acting in the American public interest nor in the interests of a global civil society.

American mainstream media, profit-driven by nature, largely fail the public interest as well. The *New York Times*, the so-called newspaper of record, is not printing all the news that's fit to print about the full spectrum of the Bush administration's activities—especially those occurring behind corporate doors or on distant battlefields. There's plenty in this new media/mental mind-management era that is out of public reach and public comment, hidden in so-called black budgets that merge intelligence, covert action, with information and psyops programs.[8] There's also plenty that we as citizens allow the United States press to get away with by not pressing Bush and other people in power about what they mean by "axis of evil" and the "defense of freedom." Whose freedom? My freedom or your freedom? Freedom for McDonnell Douglas or Exxon Mobil? The American people need public-interest media in which we can better learn about, debate, and challenge the policies that curtail civil liberties at home and put innocent people in harm's way abroad.

I remember hearing Representative Henry Hyde ask, shortly after 9/11, "How is it that the country that invented Hollywood and Madison Avenue engendered so much hatred?" That question seemed to sail around the Internet as an example of a nation of leaders out of step with how others see us. Hyde, the chairman of the House International Relations Committee, introduced the Freedom Promotion Act of 2002, which later died in the Senate. In his statement to the press about this new legislation, which would have revitalized and reformed public diplomacy and foreign broadcasting efforts, he remarked, "If any nation has been a greater force for good in the long and tormented history of this world, I am unaware of it. We have guarded whole continents from conquest, showered aid on distant lands, sent thousands of youthful idealists to remote and often inhospitable areas to help the world's forgotten. Why, then, when we read or listen to descriptions of America in the foreign press do we so often seem to be entering a fantasyland of hatred?"[9]

Obviously, an echo chamber of statements about America's being the greatest country on earth is counterproductive to improving American relations with the world. Has Rep. Hyde actually sat down with some members of the foreign press who criticize the United States to get an accurate measure of the source of that criticism? It shouldn't surprise the Bush administration at all that the world's perception of the United States is, at best, mixed. No government, including our own, is immune from engaging in actions that harm, especially since governments are often driven by their own narrow self-interests. But the United States propaganda message begs to differ:... "No, really, we're the greatest nation on earth,"—perhaps, in P.T. Barnum's view, the greatest show on earth. The world's people and its press have long become weary of this refrain.

The United States propaganda war has expanded over time. While we bemoan the fact that propaganda is infiltrating the media today, during World War II the newsreels produced by the press were almost indistinguishable from the military's objective. Recall the now legendary Eisenhower outgoing speech of 1961, in which he warned that our country must "guard against the acquisition of unwarranted influence, whether sought or unsought, by the military-industrial complex." He's famous for having added the "military-industrial complex" to our vocabulary, but if he were alive today, I think he would perhaps add another M: since his time, the landscape of power and control has become a military-media-industrial complex. The military and the media absorb the bulk of available resources for research technology. Anything that's invested in information technology in the United States is applied in military and media sectors before filtering down to the mass consumer society. Citizens are the last to gain public access to any new technology that will make our lives freer and make it easier for us to politically participate in and challenge the power establishments.

Wartime propaganda in the twentieth century and beyond has always been impacted by the American motion-picture industry and the American press. Imagine the propaganda potential of film with a captive audience of hundreds of millions in the early part of the last century alone?. In Philip Taylor's book, *Munitions of the Mind*, he describes the massive film operation set up by the Office of War Information, the genesis to the independent United States Information Agency, just months after the Pearl Harbor attack. What we used to call the United States War Department—now the Department of Defense—annually spent over $50 million on film production during World War II to propagate the message of the war both here and overseas. The famous Hollywood film director Frank Capra (*Mr. Smith Goes to Washington*, *It's a Wonderful Life*), became Major Frank Capra during the war and was asked by General George C. Marshall to make the *Why We Fight* documentary war series. The free press is comprised of people like you and me, who are just as subject to a swell of patriotism and ultra-nationalism as is anyone else. We like to idealize the free press, believing that it will truly separate out its nationalistic bent about a story and report objectively, but World War I and World War II were characterized by the American press as the War to End All Wars and The Good War respectively. The American press worked in tandem with the military objectives of the United States government as part of its sense of duty to the country in wartime.

Today, propaganda infiltration of the media system is more intense than ever. One cannot turn to the Internet as a source of "the absolute truth," since the Internet functions as an open media system and is subject to the same rumormongering and gossip as the *National Enquirer*. The Internet, as the media and democracy scholar Robert McChesney notes, is also being colonized by the corporate landscape. The elite media outlets have gradually replaced the democratic pursuit of truth with the undemocratic placement and distribution of planted publicity stories. As John Stauber, coauthor of *Toxic Sludge is Good for You*, remarks about the United States public relations industry, most of what we, the audience, thinks is news is just P. R. that is pitched to program producers by the publicity department of an entity with a vested interest in seeing that person or idea promoted. The public-relations guru Fraser Seitel talked about the P. R. process with Bill O'Reilly of the Fox News Channel. The discussion turned to was whether or not Rosie O'Donnell had tainted her reputation by publicly attacking the publishers of her failing *Rosie* magazine. Seitel was asked what first piece of advice he would give O'Donnell if she were to call on him. He said, "First, pay me." His honest statement spoke to exactly what's going on in the media/propaganda system. It's pay to play. The public often doesn't know what is going on because we're just the spectators in the crowd watching the gladiators go at it. "Will

Rosie cave to the public pressure?" becomes newsworthy and functions as a propaganda technique to assign a sense of meaning to the meaningless. It filters up to the highest echelons of our government, where presidents make such statements as, "They hate freedom," and get away with that. As long as we continue to allow the media to function as a manipulative mind manager without fear or disfavor, we'll continue to see the brain-numbing effects of a society underexposed to real information and analysis, rendered incapable of critical judgment and social resistance.

It's not enough, however, to say that the media are a propaganda system and to point fingers at all the media owners and employees for being manipulators of news. Part of the challenge for the news reader is to distinguish the true facts from spin and opining. In the American media system, editorializing is theoretically positioned on the editorial pages, thus giving the reader the false sense of security that opinions and persuasion are not part of the regular news. Since the onslaught of twenty-four-hour cable news programs and increased competition for the public's attention both in print and broadcast, the American media system is embedding facts with opinions and placing editorial comments and news analyses on the front page. In contrast, Great Britain has never assumed such a distinction between facts and opinions. The public's dilemma is to know how to consume the news with an ability to extract opinion from the simple facts and evidence.

Most media scholars today would recommend that the public accept the fact that objective reporting is more textbook than reality and that news media outlets are likely to expand integration of voice, spin, and slant to the packaging of information. The best solution to the fact/opinion dilemma is to acquire more diverse information across the ideological and geological divide. If you find yourself relying on one source of information for the news, whether right or left, you are likely to be exposed to more opinion that reinforces rather than challenges your own.

At a deeper level of information manipulation, government-sponsored propaganda programs have long been effective, deadly so. Walter Lippmann, considered the father of modern American journalism, was also a writer of propaganda leaflets during World War I. He saw how easily people could fall for lies small and big, particularly captured prisoners of war who were easily manipulated by their captors. Lippmann became so disillusioned by the public's inability to analyze policy that he wrote *The Phantom Public*, in which he basically claimed that the public had no role to play in addressing important questions of state because the media system created a pseudoreality of stereotypes and emotional impressions along with facts. The public is easily manipulated, not because we're necessarily dumb, but because we're ignorant. We don't have the necessary tools to counter the propaganda. We don't teach effective media or information literacy or even advertising literacy—the surround-sound propaganda of our society—in our schools or universities, and this omission is both by design and by demand. Good old-fashioned gumshoe-style journalism is almost nonexistent at Cal State Fullerton, where I teach full-time. Our journalism concentration is on the decline, while advertising, public relations, and marketing (spin, style, and the Big Sell) are proliferating. You cannot blame the students for choosing concentrations that are in higher demand, but such demand reinforces the propaganda infiltration of the press and media—that mythical Fourth Estate that was set up to both protect the public from institutional exploitation and inform the public of all matters necessary to good governance.

Advertising is both propaganda and our current society's propaganda distributor. The U.S. Army, like all our armed forces, has become very sophisticated about its target audience—young people of color who are struggling against the odds in this economy and need training and skills to get ahead. Aspects of modern warfare look like a video game, so why not present it as such? It's no coincidence that universities like USC's Institute for Creative Technologies, with its close ties to the Hollywood film industry, have been working closely with the military to develop cutting-edge virtual-reality technology from the entertainment and game-development industries to help train the modern soldier and future soldier. There are billions of resources that go into maintaining a modern military like that of the United States. It's not all tanks and soldiers. Much of it is technology geared toward persuasion and information management. Since we don't have a draft and have to rely on an all-volunteer armed force, the military has to continue to come up with clever ways to work through all the advertising clutter and capture their declining audience. The "Army of One" campaign worked with MTV and VH1 to produce video diaries—a sort of Real World Kabul instead of a Real World Las Vegas. Since the techniques are similar, with popular music overlays and quick-cut shots, to the viewer both look the same. Will the MTV generation understand the content of these military video diaries better when viewing them in a format with which the viewers are familiar? Yes, but these activities are also symptomatic of the triumph of the image and media over content. Much of our media now are so image-rich and content-poor that they just serve to capture the eye, manipulate our emotions, and short-circuit our impulses. The propaganda and advertising industries therefore function increasingly like adult obedience industries. They instruct their audiences in how to feel and what to think, and increasing numbers of people seem to accept and follow the cues without question.

There's still plenty about the information war that is hidden from view, particularly the nastiest stuff, like psyops and psywar operations that target inscrutable enemies, wherever they may be. Psyops (psychological operations) and psywar (psychological operations warfare) have a combat function that targets both friendly and enemy audiences in support of a battle mission, like the U.S. Air Force C-130 "Commando Solo" aircraft that broadcast radio messages warning Afghan and Iraqi citizens to avoid collaboration with enemy soldiers. Unlike our alleged open-media systems, these operations are neither balanced nor complete by design and are therefore kept separate from public-diplomacy and public-affairs missions. Much is going on in a manner that is nevertheless "hiding in plain sight." It's as if the U.S. government and U.S. media, all too aware that we as a society lack a critical approach to our consumption of news, present information in increasingly banal pro-government terms with a little counterintelligence and reactionary history thrown in the mix.

We often hear the mid- to late 1960s described as a watershed moment for social change, not just in the United States but also worldwide. It was also a time when great hope for change in social institutions was quickly snuffed out. Assassinations of visionaries for change were rampant—from Robert Kennedy and Martin Luther King, Jr., to Malcolm X. The FBI-led COINTEL (counterintelligence) programs subverted the momentum of social change, and the fabricated Gulf of Tonkin incident in 1964 increased American involvement in Vietnam. The worldwide student movement of 1968 was effectively countered by elites in the nation and the media, who were threatened by masses of young people questioning "the system.". Fast forward to today, and if you want to learn about a truly investigative role by an elite press, you have to watch a old film like *All the President's Men*. Young gung-ho types at the *Washington Post* or *New York Times* haven't replaced Bob Woodward, Carl Bernstein, and Daniel Ellsberg. No, instead, we hear the reactionary refrain that the "liberal" *New York Times* is being too hard on the Bush administration, as if that were the extent of our criticism continuum. I suppose it's the best we can do as frogs slowly heating in the boiling pot. The question remains, will we jump out before everything reaches the boiling point? The combination of the "No Debate on Iraq" phenomenon and the Bush doctrine's mandate to conduct preemptive strikes wherever and whenever—that may be that boiling point. But I'm not sure if we'll have the energy to jump out and save ourselves.

"Media Collusion and the Rise of the Fourth Reich"

If you once forfeit the confidence of your fellow citizens, you can never regain their respect and esteem. It is true that you may fool all the people some of the time; you can even fool some of the people all of the time; but you can't fool all of the people all of the time.

—ABRAHAM LINCOLN

□ □ □

ON JULY 30, 2003, I participated in a public forum entitled, "Media Collusion and the Rise of the Fourth Reich," held at the University of British Columbia in Vancouver. The *American Heritage Dictionary of the English Language* defines collusion as "a secret agreement between two or more parties for a fraudulent, illegal, or deceitful purpose." What is implied in the title of the public forum is essentially the melding of the state and media with the values and goals of militarism and authoritarianism.

Since the end of World War II, the United States media have embraced the assumptions of the national security state and official Washington. Is this close cooperation between the United States news media and the United States government over national-security issues the result of an overt conspiracy to keep the public ill-informed about sensitive matters? Or is it the result of an array of complex and subtle sociological forces? I would argue that it is somewhere in between. I do not believe, having worked for the federal government in Washington, D.C. for two years, that the United States is using all the authoritarian tools that were used by the Third Reich, but the United States certainly is using some of them.

Walter Lippman wrote, "Without some form of censorship, propaganda in the strictest sense of the word is impossible. In order to conduct a propaganda there must be some barrier between the public and the event. Access to the real environment must be limited, before anyone can create a pseudo-environment that he thinks is wise or desirable."

In that quote, the father of modern American journalism lays out the two essential tools in modern media collusion with the state: censorship and propaganda. Censorship ends the free flow of information so essential for democracy and makes dissent less likely. Propaganda injects false or misleading information into the media in order to influence the behavior of populations here and abroad. How does censorship operate in news organizations? News organizations often willingly collude with efforts to censor because media owners are members of the political elite themselves and therefore share the goals and outcomes of government leaders. Profit ranks higher than truth telling in the minds of media owners and many of their employees. Now, certainly this attitude doesn't apply to every employee, but should some idealist buck the system, s/he'll pay for it, while those who play along and follow the rules will benefit directly and rise in the ranks. One recent case in point is MSNBC journalist Ashleigh Banfield, who gave a public lecture at Kansas State University on April 24, 2003, in which she blasted American journalists for their subjective complicity in the war in Iraq:

There are horrors that were completely left out of this war. So was this journalism or was this coverage? There is a grand difference between journalism and coverage, and getting access does not mean you're getting the story, it just means you're getting one more arm or leg of the story. And that's what we got, and it was a glorious, wonderful picture that had a lot of people watching and a lot of advertisers excited about cable news. But it wasn't journalism, because I'm not so sure that we in America are hesitant to do this again, to fight another war, because it looked like a glorious and courageous and so successful terrific endeavor, and we got rid of a horrible leader: We got rid of a dictator, we got rid of a monster, but we didn't see what it took to do that. ...

[W]e really don't know from this latest adventure from the American military what this thing looked like and why perhaps we should never do it again. The other thing is that so many voices were silent in this war. We all know what happened to Susan Sarandon for speaking out, and her husband, and we all know that this is not the way Americans truly want to be. Free speech is a wonderful thing, it's what we fight for, but the minute it's unpalatable we fight against it for some reason.[10]

This speech prompted a statement from an NBC spokeswoman, who told reporters on Monday, April 28: "She and we [NBC] both agreed that she didn't intend to demean the work of her colleagues, and she will choose her words more carefully in the future."[11]

The dominance of censorship and propaganda is a triumph of authoritarian over democratic values. During times of national crisis, like the Cold War and the current War on Terrorism, authoritarianism takes precedent over such civil liberties as the democratic process and the rights protected by the First Amendment. The general trend since the mid-twentieth century has been away from openness and toward increasing government secrecy, coupled with a rise in contempt among policymakers for the American public's right to know. Recall the "lone dissenter" Representative Barbara Lee, the sole member of the Congress who voted against the following resolution on September 14, 2001: "The President is authorized to use all necessary and appropriate force against those nations, organizations, or persons he determined planned, authorized, or aided the terrorist attacks that occurred on September 11, 2001 or harbored such organizations or persons." Her rationale was based on the words of the Bishop at the National Cathedral earlier that same day: "We must not become the evil we deplore." Where were the other voices to protect the checks and balances' function of the three branches of government? They were silent and complicit.

During the most recent war with Iraq, much was made about the close ties between the two main coalition allies, Britain and the United States. Since World War I, the United States has borrowed and adapted many of the methods of British political intelligence that were first developed by the English aristocracy to manage its global empire. Most of our secrecy classification system in the United States is based on the British model. Britain has also long been a master of propaganda and deception. The British authors Phillip Knightly and Philip Taylor have shown in their work how the British propaganda machine of World War I inspired later efforts by the Nazi Propaganda Minister Joseph Goebbels.[12] Interestingly, Britain, with its Official Secrets Act, has never shared the American traditional ideals about the freedom of the press and the public's right to know. Nevertheless, the steady erosion of these ideals in the United States can be traced in part to the special relationship and mutual admiration between the United States and Great Britain.

Another long American tradition is the tendency of American news media and national security communities to share personnel, what is often called the revolving-door syndrome that leads to collusion and group think. The intelligence and news media communities have much in common: both are interested in the gathering of information, although one community over the other is able to more readily distribute that information, at least in principle. Journalists have the liberty of traveling in hostile territories, a freedom that allows intelligence agents to sometimes masquerade as journalists. Finally, propaganda can be more easily injected into news from the inside than from the outside. Using CIA documents, the American reporter Carl Bernstein was able to identify more than 400 American journalists who secretly carried out CIA assignments over a twenty-five-year period between 1945 and 1970.[13] Among media executives who cooperated with the CIA were the president of CBS, William Paley, Henry Luce of *Time*, Arthur Hays Sulzberger of the *New York Times*, and James Copley of the Copley News Service. The most valued CIA assets were the *New York Times*, CBS, and Time, Inc. The *New York Times* alone provided cover to the CIA for at least ten operatives between 1950 and 1966. Bernstein found that those journalists who played along with the CIA by signing secrecy agreements were most likely to succeed in their careers because the CIA connection gave them access to the best stories. The journalists and their CIA handlers often shared the same educational background and the same ideal that both were serving the national-security interests of the United States. Included in the many examples of the intelligence community/media revolving door are: (1) the former CIA director Richard Helms (mid-1960s to early 1970s) was once a UPI wire service correspondent. (2) William Casey, the CIA director under Ronald Reagan was once chief counsel and a board member at CapCities, which absorbed ABC News in Reagan's second term. (3) Two prominent journalists, Edward R. Murrow and Carl Rowan, served as directors of the U.S. Information Agency under Kennedy, while the NBC Nightly News reporter John Chancellor was director of the government international propaganda radio service, Voice of America, under L. B. Johnson. (4) The first deputy director of the NSA, Joseph H. Ream, had previously worked as executive vice president of CBS, and after NSA, he returned to CBS without disclosing his association with the supersecretive agency. (5) Perhaps best known is the World War I propaganda apparatus known as the Committee on Public Information chaired by the progressive journalist George Creel with the assistance of Lord Northcliffe, owner of the *Times* of London and the *Daily Mail*, and a central figure in the massive British propaganda effort of World War I.

The point to be made is that the intelligence and media communities are and have been closely affiliated with each other. What such collusion leads to is censorship, such as when Arthur Sulzberger prevented his reporter Sydney Gruson from covering the United States–backed overthrow of the Guatemalan government in 1954 at the direct request of Sulzberger's good friend Allen Dulles.[14] All of us would like to think that such cozy relationships are a thing of the past, something that died with the winds of the Cold War and that both the CIA and the news media today swear off the use of American journalists as spies or agents "except in some unforeseeable emergency where lives are at stake."[15] Given the perpetual need for manipulation of news content and the reality that national security threats never disappear, it is highly unlikely that such powerful alliances have just magically disappeared.

Domestic propaganda in news benefited from a major resurgence during the Reagan-Bush years and has lasted to the present. One famous atrocity story under Reagan involved the "yellow rain" episode, in which the Soviet Union—the source of great evil—was charged with using a mysterious yellow chemical against villagers in Laos, Cambodia, and Afghanistan. The ominous substance turned out to be bee excrement but this discovery was made long after the United States media had reported the atrocity claims. As Norman Solomon and Martin Lee wrote about Reagan-era propaganda strategies:

> The pattern was set early in his administration: leak a scare story about foreign enemies, grab the headlines. If, much later, reporters poke holes in the cover story, so what? The truth will receive far less attention than the original lie, and by then another round of falsehoods will be dominating the headlines.[16]

Once started, a good atrocity story is often unstoppable, as was noted by John McArthur of *Harper's* about the Gulf War news coverage:

> Once bad information burrows into what's traditionally known at newspapers as 'the morgue' (the clippings file organized by subject and name in the newspaper library), it gets repeated over and over again. Newspaper reporters are perpetually in a hurry, and their principal historical sources when

writing a story on deadline are past stories from their own paper. Like a computer virus, inaccuracy infects a newspaper morgue (the morgues at large newspapers are now mostly computerized), and it can sometimes take years to cleanse the system.[17]

An acceptable form of domestic propaganda embedded into news media was utilized in the war in Afghanistan and the war with Iraq. In the mid-1990s, the U.S. Air Force specially designed a propaganda and psychological warfare aircraft, called *Commando Solo* that was capable of overriding domestic media broadcasts (radio and TV) and substituting outside content of any kind, true or false. In April 2003, Commando Solo was used to rebroadcast United States media nightly newscasts featuring Tom Brokaw and Peter Jennings into Iraq in order to demonstrate to the newly liberated Iraqi people what free media broadcasts look like. A more sinister version of domestic propaganda insertion is CIA sponsorship of global media, including Radio Free Europe, Radio Liberty (Cuba), Radio Free Asia, and numerous print publications, such as *Prevves* (France), *Der Monat* (Germany), *El Mundo Nuevo* (Latin America), *Quiet and Thought* (India), *Argumenten* (Sweden), and *La Prensa* (Nicaragua).

If the use of propaganda as a joint venture of the United States government and commercial media is now so routine and pervasive, how can we believe the news we consume? Having access to in-depth news is crucial to upholding our democratic traditions. The commercial media may think that they can help us distinguish between objective truth, subjective opinion, and downright deception, but history shows us that they are now as much part of the problem as they are the part of the solution. As the citizens did with *Pravda* in the former Soviet Union, so too can Americans learn to read between the lines of the official story. If we want the full story, we have to seek other sources—we have to turn to our own samizdat[18] literature online and in alternative media.

Contrary to the needs of an informed public, the interests of the government, big business, and media increasing blur and merge. In 1985, General Electric, one of the largest military arms merchants on the planet, acquired NBC, a trade that at the time raised eyebrows about NBC's ability to provide objective news coverage on any subject in which GE might have an interest. CBS was previously owned by Westinghouse, another arms merchant, until it was sold to Viacom. ABC is owned by Disney, and CNN is owned by Time Warner (which includes the Warner Brothers studio). Both Disney and Warner Brothers were long cooperative partners with the government during World War II, producing domestic propaganda in the guise of entertainment for the masses. As we all know, the merging of military and media corporations has been accompanied by an overall decline and concentration in the number of companies that control the news. As Ben Bagdikian wrote in his book *The Media Monopoly*, this interlocking nature of corporate news networks has led to a decline in in-depth investigative reporting of military and nuclear-power stories.[19]

The interlocked interests of government, big business, and media are likely to remain a formidable and dominant force in American politics and foreign policy. What should concern us is that when commercial and government interests that tend toward secrecy and perception management, rather than reflecting traditional democratic ideals of freedom of speech and a free press, end up on the same team, we need to recall the words of President Eisenhower: "We should take nothing for granted."

In the July/August 2003 issue of the *Columbia Journalism Review*, its managing editor, Brent Cunningham questions whether the American tradition of objectivity in news (promoting fairness and balance) has made United States journalists passive recipients of news, particularly information from official sources, like government and corporation elites. One case cited is the October 2001 memo from then CNN chairman Walter Isaacson while the war in Afghanistan was under way. Isaacson sent a memo to all CNN foreign correspondents telling them to seek "balance" in all their reports of Afghan casualties by reminding their audience that such hardship or death came in response to the terrorist attacks of September 11. Cunningham reports in "Re-thinking Objectivity" that an intern called newspaper editors during the war in Iraq to see whether letters to the editor were running for or against the war and was told by the editor of *The Tennessean* that although letters were 70 percent against the war, the editor chose to run more prowar letters so that they wouldn't be accused by some of their readers of being biased.

Objectivity, or its pursuit, persists in the United States because it separates American journalism from the chaotic partisan journalism of our European allies. Cunningham warns, however, that pursuing objectivity can trip us up on the way to truth. Objectivity excuses lazy reporting. If you're on deadline and all you have is "both sides of the story," that's often good enough. It's not that such stories laying out the parameters of the debate have no value for readers, but too often, in our obsession with, as *The Washington Post's* Bob Woodward puts it, "the latest," we fail to push the story, incrementally, toward a deeper understanding of what is true and what is false.[20]

More troubling, Cunningham notes that objectivity "exacerbates our tendency to rely on official sources." Striking a balance, fundamental to a principle of objectivity, often means getting the "he said" and the "she said" side of the equation. This often leads to phenomenal media dependence on or collusion with the official story. The *Tyndall Report* by the media analyst Andrew Tyndall analyzed 414 stories on Iraq from the Major Three (ABC, CBS, and NBC) between September 2002 and February 2003 and found that all but 34 stories originated at three government agencies—The White House, the Pentagon, and the State Department.[21] Why such dependence? Mostly time. The nonstop news cycle in major media and the new media threat from the Internet and Shout TV on cable has left reporters with less time to dig deeper in stories. This development encourages greater reliance on official sources of information that can deliver "the goods" quickly and efficiently.

When the United States and the world were debating a war with Iraq in the fall of 2002, not one official in the Bush administration had much interest in discussing the aftermath of a war. More important was to mount a full-court press for a preemptive attack. The details of the aftermath would be worked out later, but the public and press attention was to push for "regime change." The consequence of the "he said" debate was that no "she said" counterbalance debate on the aftermath of war took place, with few exceptions.[22] According to the *Tyndall Report*, of 574 stories about Iraq on the ABC, CBS, and NBC evening news aired between Bush's address to the United Nations on September 12, 2002, and March 7, 2003, just 12 stories dealt with the aftermath of the war with Iraq. As Cunningham asks, "If something important is being ignored, doesn't the press have an obligation to force our elected officials to address it?" Not if that press is of the same mindset and ideology of those with whom it confers about information, and not if the ignored story is going to upend an otherwise good relationship between reporter and source. The *New York Times* carried a headline on November 25, 2002, that read, "CBS Staying Silent in Debate About Women Joining Augusta," a reference to the network's coverage of The Masters Golf Championship at Augusta National Country Club, which has a policy of excluding women from membership. There was, as Cunningham noted, never a headline that read "Bush Still Mum on Aftermath." Was the aftermath of war in a foreign country any less important or newsworthy than a domestic disturbance on the links in Georgia?

Media omission, like media collusion, is illustrative of a sameness in the American newsroom, which lacks diversity not only in ethnic, racial, and gender categories, but perhaps more important, a lack of diversity in upbringing and outlook. You won't get the working-class Irish coming through the door for an interview as often as the Ivy League–educated pup journalist with upper-class sensibilities. This attitude creates a bias born of class, race, and socioeconomic heritage. Couple this with a media bias toward conflict, the herd mentality, and event-driven coverage, and you've got the makings of a reinforced passivity in public media consumption. The charge of liberal bias is overstated, according to James Carey, a scholar at Columbia University and author of *Television and the Press*; he notes that "there is a bit of a reformer in anyone who enters journalism. And reformers are always going to make conservatives uncomfortable to an extent because conservatives, by and large, want to preserve the status quo."[23]

So we must ask ourselves, as we often do, "What is there to be done?" A few modest proposals for liberating alternatives in media follow: First, I reinforce the first proposal from Cunningham for rethinking objectivity in American journalism: "Journalists (and journalism) must acknowledge, humbly and publicly, that what we do is far more subjective and far less detached than the aura of objectivity implies—

47

and the public wants to believe." Secondly, we must recognize and confront the myths we live by, namely, several that I've addressed here. One myth is of a supposed adversarial relationship between government and the media. This is a myth that is convenient for both communities and is sustained for mutual benefit. Another common myth is that overt censorship in news organizations does not exist. Overt censorship does exist, and it has a historical precedent, the result of benefits that reporters receive in their career advancement, as well as benefits that the government receives in return for media complicity in its efforts to mislead the public through domestic propaganda (for example, regarding Saddam's weapons of mass destruction). We must acknowledge the enormous reliance in corporate media on spin and official versions of the truth. The United States government relies on a form of censorship known as censorship at the source, those unnamed official sources of the news that we often see referenced on the front pages of our newspapers. This method keeps both journalists and the public in the dark. Finally, the trend is toward greater consolidation of the media and less open and democratic government or media. The twenty-four-hour news cycle requires constant feeding, a hunger that advertising and pre-packaged publicity sources of news are only too happy to nourish. In the federal government, the largest public-relations division is inside the Pentagon, where government public-relations specialists provide M-F feeds to the national media. "Embedded" reporters didn't just accompany the military to the battle in Iraq, they also sat regularly for prearranged briefings from Donald Rumsfeld, Torie Clarke, and Ari Fleischer. In the corporate media environment today, the best journalist is increasingly the dutiful journalist, who understands that symbiotic relationship between official channels of information sources and the news-story product. Long gone are the days of independent journalists like George Seldes, who would have gladly been kicked out of his first Washington press briefing in exchange for the neighborhood goings on back home.

What this media reality means for the rest of us is that media activism is and must become a larger part of our being citizens in the world. Given what we know now about media collusion with the centers of power, we have no choice but to create our own independent media while we confront, cajole, and analyze the forces of government and big business that dominate our mental landscape.

In the Beginning, There Was George

□□□

I DO NOT SPEAK OF THIS GEORGE, otherwise known as 43, or even that George, known as 4341. The George of whom I write is George Creel. George Creel was to President Woodrow Wilson what Karl Rove—"Bush's Brain"—is to President George W. Bush. George Creel authored a book with one of the longest titles on record and certainly one of the most bombastic: *How We Advertised America: The First Telling of the Amazing Story of the Committee on Public Information that Carried the Gospel of Americanism to Every Corner of the Globe.* Could anyone but an American have written a book with such an amazing title? The early-twentieth-century George Creel has much to teach the early-twenty-first about how to win the propaganda war for hearts and minds.

It was 1917. Creel, an American journalist and editor and, more importantly, an F.O.W. (Friend of Woodrow), convinced President Wilson that what the country needed was not a Committee on Censorship to control the mind of the over-whelmingly pacifistic and apathetic American public's entry into World War I. No indeed, George Creel had the clever idea then to create a Committee on Public Information "for the production and dissemination as widely as possible of the truth about America's participation in the war."[24] The CPI was an ad hoc committee whose membership included the leading persuasion and propaganda experts of the day, the avowed dean of American journalism, Walter Lippmann, and Edward Bernays, the grandfather of American public relations. But it was George Creel, that early George, who commanded the spotlight and knew that to win the Great War, he had to convince the American people, like George number 43 does in the first war of the twenty-first century, that this war was a fight over ideas and values more than a fight over land, people, and resources. Controlling public opinion was a major force during World War I as it was to become in World War II and now in the War on Terror. The issues of the day would be fought in the media and mental mindfields of men and women as well as on the minefields of battle. Creel wrote of his mission:

> In no degree was the Committee an agency of censorship, a machinery of concealment or repression. Its emphasis throughout was on the open and the positive. At no point did it seek or exercise authorities under those war laws that limited the freedom of speech and press. In all things, from first to last, without halt or change, it was a plain publicity proposition, a vast enterprise in salesmanship, the world's greatest adventures in advertising...We did not call it propaganda, for that word, in German hands, had come to be associated with deceit and corruption. Our effort was educational and informative throughout, for we had such confidence in our case as to feel that no other argument was needed than the simple, straightforward presentation of the facts.[25]

What does George Creel teach us now about the War on Terrorism? In order to win the information war then, the administration, through Creel's Committee, had to convince the population that the Great War was not the war of the Wilson administration, but rather a war of one hundred million people: "What we had to have was no mere surface unity, but a passionate belief in the justice of America's cause that moulds the people of the United States into one white-hot mass instinct of fraternity, devotion, courage, and deathless determination. The *war-will*, the will-to-win, of a democracy depends upon the degree to which each one of all the people of that democracy can concentrate and consecrate body and soul and spirit in the supreme effort of service and sacrifice. What had to be driven home was that all business was the nation's business, and every task a common task for a single purpose."[26]

To George Creel, the peace and labor movements of the early twentieth century created unacceptable conditions for generating a mass warmaking mindset.[27] To turn a pacifist and neutral populace into one white-hot mass instinct, Creel made the Committee a totally integrative enterprise, with "no part of the Great War machinery that we did not touch, no medium of appeal that we did not employ."[28] This included print, radio, motion pictures, telegraph, and cable messages and worldwide circulation of President Wilson's official addresses from Teheran to Tokyo, posters, and signboards, along with a volunteer service corps of 75,000 speakers known as the Four-Minute Men, who worked in 5,200 communities and made a total of 755,190 speeches, with "every one having the carry of shrapnel."[29]

The Committee on Public Information was in the business of mobilizing world public opinion in support of American participation in the war. By the time of World War II, the United States government and military institutions were fully engaged in an all-out information war that built upon the efforts put forth by the ambitious George Creel.

The Bush administration's war on terror is in the same business of mobilizing mass public opinion both here and abroad. There is no government support for alternatives to the administration's war on terrorism. An early sign of this Creel-like mobilization of the mind came in the form of a September 27, 2001, *New York Times* op-ed article by Defense Secretary Donald Rumsfeld: "Some believe the first casualty of any war is the truth. But in this war, the first victory must be to tell the truth. Even the vocabulary of this war will be different...forget about exit strategies, we're looking at a sustained engagement that carries no deadlines."[30] That sustained engagement with no exit deadline would employ an ambitious information and propaganda effort not seen since George Creel's Committee laid a foundation for advertising America in wartime.

In the early months of the October 2001 ground offensive in Afghanistan, the propaganda war began to heat up and the truth about war was, in fact, becoming its first casualty. The public diplomacy section of the U.S. State Department, under the leadership of Charlotte Beers, was beginning its global task of reshaping the image of America through international diplomatic efforts. Beers, a former Madison Avenue advertising executive, was assigned the most ambitious branding assignment of her life—repackaging America's image so to "sell" the war against terrorism to the Islamic world. In a foreign media reaction report issued in late October 2001, the State Department had to acknowledge that the United States had a global image and credibility problem not exclusive to Osama Bin Laden and the Taliban in Afghanistan.[31] Growing anti-Americanism came from a global perception, however true or not, that America exhibited a "do as we say, not as we do" bias in its policymaking. Even advertising and brand experts like Beers would have to acknowledge that nations are judged by what they do, not by how they would like to be seen, with the United States being no exception. The United States seemed to be losing the information war because it was having a problem pushing its global do-gooder image in light of its militaristic foreign policy and its with-us-or-against-us rhetoric. But Uncle Ben's Rice and disposable razors don't create credibility or image problems to be overcome the way a nation like the United States does vis-à-vis its foreign policy.[32] When former U.S. Ambassador Richard Holbrooke told an audience at Michigan State University that Bin Laden was able to release—with strategic timing—a "Hollywood quality video" in praise of the September 11 attackers, it seemed that the world's superpower was losing its communications war to a guy in a cave.[33]

By November 2001, it was clear that America's new war would have to emphasize imagery as much as weaponry. The information war, a form of soft power projection, would be key to defeating Osama Bin Laden's Al Qaeda network. Bin Laden's advantage was in waging classic guerrilla warfare, where one fights in four dimensions—air, land, sea, and information. If the United States were to prevail, then it had to shift its orientation from a strict bombs-and-bullets approach to one that also used words and images. In the new war on terror, images were seen as more important than bombing accuracy—a shift from the Gulf War where the image and the bomb were equally deployed. The *New York Times* reported in a 4,200 word front-page story that top United States officials, working with the British government, were mounting "what may be the most ambitious wartime communications effort since World War II...a first step in a broader campaign to create a twenty-first-century version of the muscular propaganda war that the United States waged in the 1940s. Matching old-fashioned patriotism to the frantic pace of modern communications, the Bush administration is trying to persuade audiences here and abroad to support the war. At the same time, it is trying to control the release of information about military intelligence and operations."[34]

In an accompanying special report called "Hearts and Minds," the administration's efforts to maintain a tight control on information about the war in Afghanistan were attributed to the fact that the United States war in Vietnam, raising unrealistic expectations about success, eroded public confidence in the government's honesty. To manage public opinion at home, the Bush administration chose to coordinate information across the upper levels of government and to utilize "Greatest Generation" icons from World War II as well as Hollywood image generators.[35]

America's emerging information war overseas was now being waged on two fronts. On one front, public-diplomacy efforts by Charlotte Beers and Richard Boucher in the State Department were designed to generate international support for U.S. policies. Dubbed by the *National Journal* "brand of the free" strategies, these long-term efforts to shift public opinion in favor of the United States included educational and cultural exchanges, advertising campaigns coordinated through the World War II–era Advertising Council, radio broadcasting, and public outreach to foreign press. A second front waged by the Department of Defense/Pentagon consisted of short-term wartime communication strategies and tactics—psychological warfare targeted at enemy forces in Afghanistan and wherever else the war against terror would employ the United States military. For the most part, the Bush administration stayed away from the term "propaganda" for these mass persuasion activities. As one former U.S. Information Agency official and director of the Public Diplomacy Institute at George Washington University, Barry Fulton, put it: "Until the mid-60s, if somebody called you a propagandist, nobody was offended. Later on it begins to have a tone of doing something underhanded."[36]

By March 2002, just six months after the launch of the American invasion and occupation of Afghanistan, the information war at home was also emerging as a battle on two fronts—a battle oriented toward both opinion control and the suppression of free speech. Within the government corridors, the Bush administration was losing its battle for control of information about new developments in the war on terror, namely, through two high-profile press leaks about the Nuclear Posture Review (NPR) and Pentagon's Office of Strategic Influence (OSI).[37] The information war on opinion and free speech intensified with the creation of several post-9/11 nonprofit organizations. These included Americans for Victory Over Terrorism (AVOT), whose intention is to "take their task to those groups and individuals who fundamentally misunderstand the nature of the war we are facing." Among those targeted by AVOT were Congressman Dennis Kucinich, chair of the Progressive Caucus and his cochair, Congresswoman Barbara Lee; Lewis Lapham, editor of *Harper's* magazine; and Robert Kuttner, editor of *The American Prospect*. AVOT's work followed from the work of the American Council of Trustees and Alumni (ACTA), which issued a November 2001 report, "Defending Civilization: How Our Universities are Failing America," that condemned dissident anti-war language propagated by liberal professors on American college campuses.[38] The co-founder of Empower America, one of the wealthiest of the right-wing Washington, D.C., think tanks and former Secretary of Education under President George Bush, Sr., (George 41) William Bennett, has said, "We do not wish to silence people," and added that AVOT plans to hold teach-ins and public education events, particularly on college campuses. Both organizations are united in their belief that the United States must retain its superpower empire for global goodness and redemption, keep military ethics and power the primary focus of the United States response to 9/11, and shout down the "morally coward liberals" on American university campuses and in Europe. If George Creel were here today, he'd be very proud of this country's single white-hot mass instinct to capture the hearts and minds of men and women both here and abroad.

When Harry Met George

AN ASSESSMENT OF THE INFORMATION WAR THEN AND NOW

It's not enough to hate your enemy. You have to understand how the two of you bring each other to deep completion.

—DON DELILLO

☐☐☐

WHICH PRESIDENT, TRUMAN OR BUSH, uttered the following words?

> One way of life is based upon the will of the majority, and is distinguished by free institutions, representative government, free elections, guarantees of personal liberty, freedom of speech and religion and freedom from political repression. The second way of life is based upon the will of a minority imposed upon the majority. It relies upon terror and repression, a controlled press and radio, fixed elections, and the suppression of personal freedoms.[39]

> The American people need to know that we're facing a different enemy than we have ever faced. This enemy hides in shadows, and has no regard for human life. This is an enemy who preys on innocent and unsuspecting people, then runs for cover. But it won't be able to run for cover forever. This is

an enemy that tries to hide. But it won't be able to hide forever. This is an enemy that thinks its harbors are safe. But they won't be safe forever. This enemy attacked not just our people, but all freedom-loving people everywhere in the world. The United States of America will use all our resources to conquer this enemy. We will rally the world. We will be patient, we will be focused, and we will be steadfast in our determination. This battle will take time and resolve. But make no mistake about it: we will win.[40]

Cold War President Harry S Truman and Terror War President George W. Bush respectively uttered these words some fifty years apart, but they speak to the same theme: a sustained war that requires winning the war on the public mind.[41] In 1950, Truman launched a "Campaign of Truth" against global communism following the outbreak of the Korean War and in response to a National Security Council report on Soviet capabilities. The United States had a clear disadvantage against Soviet propaganda capabilities, which were potent and far reaching. Truman decided to launch an American counteroffensive but couldn't call it " propaganda" if it wanted to avoid connotations that came with the word—connotations of manipulation, lies, and totalitarian control. In an April 20, 1950, speech before the American Society of Newspaper Editors, Truman launched his truth campaign. In his book, *Truth is our Weapon*, Truman's speechwriter and former Assistant Secretary of State Edward Barrett, wrote: "There was one major thing wrong with the speech: it was sure to cause headlines such as 'Truman Declares Propaganda War.' Happily, a new phrase came to mind. The American offensive was naturally to be based upon truth. Therefore, I suggested that the President call for a 'Campaign of Truth.'"[42] Truman peppered his speech with freedom and truth, the glittering generalities of our propaganda era:

> We have tremendous advantages in the struggle for men's minds and loyalties. We have truth and freedom on our side. The appeal of free institutions and self-government springs from the deepest and noblest aspirations of mankind. It is based on every man's desire for liberty and opportunity. It is based on every man's wish to be self-reliant and to shape his own destiny.[43]

Congress eventually appropriated $121 million toward the Truth Campaign, and an increased expenditure on military propaganda (psywar and psyops) allowed it to become the information component of a massive growth in armaments. Truman's search for truth followed an April 14, 1950, policy report, "NSC 68: United States Objectives and Programs for National Security," which linked Soviet propaganda to global domination. It was said then, as is being said now, that the enemy was "winning" the propaganda war and that America had to act.[44] After September 11, 2001, Rep. Henry Hyde gave voice to a rhetorical question that was on his mind and perhaps the minds of many Americans, "How is it possible that the government of the country that invented Hollywood and Madison Avenue [modern advertising] can't tell its story overseas?"[45] In 1950, A Crusade for Freedom was launched, to promote the ability of "freedom-loving peoples" in Eastern Europe to shake off the Soviet yoke and to present them with objective news and reporting through the newly created Radio Free Europe. On November 7, 2001, the United States House, to help win the information war, passed the Radio Free Afghanistan Bill. The bill's cosponsor, Rep. Ed Royce declared,

"The Taliban and the terrorists they are harboring use propaganda and censorship to maintain power. They must be countered. It's time we gave ourselves a microphone."[46] Radio Free Afghanistan is now performing its broadcasting functions as a surrogate of Radio Free Europe/Radio Liberty. The Campaign of Truth and Freedom, continues.

Propaganda is defined as any organized or concerted group effort or movement to spread a particular doctrine or a system of doctrines or principles. It is mass persuasion with a purpose that advantages the sender. It's essentially a neutral set of techniques that derives its positive or negative effects from specific application of these techniques. Three important characteristics of propaganda are that (1) it is intentional and purposeful, designed to incite a particular reaction or action in the target audience; (2) it is advantageous to the propagandist or sender (which is why advertising, public relations, and political campaigns are considered forms of propaganda; and (3) it is usually one-way and informational (as in a mass media campaign), as opposed to two-way and interactive communication.

President George W. Bush became an effective commander-in-chief of propaganda because of his ability to frame the war on terrorism in vivid and simplistic either/or terms. "The propagandist strives for simplicity and vividness, coupled with speed and broad impact. He stimulates popular emotional drives...in so doing, he must for the most part bypass factual discussion and debate of any sort."[47]

The Bush administration is now fighting an information war on two fronts—an international war on terrorism and a domestic war on American minds and public opinion. This is illustrated in the propaganda environment that drives the major United States media coverage and parrots the administration control and presentation of the facts in the War on

Terror. A fundamental routine follows five simple steps: (1) Select the Issue—Terrorism. This choice is easily made; we have the graphic footage of our national symbols of finance and military superiority being attacked. Thousands of lives are lost and hundreds of rescuers perish in pursuit of the injured. We must respond. We must take action. We need to uproot international terrorists in their efforts to override freedom and liberty. (2) Build your case. Bush's September 20, 2001, speech declared a new war on terrorism, coupled with the almost total consensus on the part of the Congress (with the exception of Rep. Barbara Lee) to allow the President to use *whatever means necessary* to fight a global war. The case-making process must employ selective facts (card stacking), a moral imperative to make the propagandist's cause appear great, noble, and honorable, or at least necessary, and to make the enemy's cause appear dastardly, uncivilized, unprincipled, or at least unnecessary. The fundamental declaration of war is framed as one as serious as the Cold War; it is nothing short of a war to defend freedom and democracy, even though the targeted enemy, Bin Laden, and Al Qaeda make no specific references to resenting American democracy or hating the American people; rather, they mention specific grievances regarding United States policy toward the Middle East and United States dominance in the region. (3) Simplification. The War on Terror requires a focus on brevity and on slogans that include common identification techniques like the Bandwagon (everybody is doing it) and Plain Folks. For example, in the Enron scandal, to sever his administration's obvious ties to the Texas conglomerate, President Bush evoked the Plain Folks Appeal, noting that his own mother-in-law lost $8,000 in Enron investments. The Bush administration's first international slogan of its war on terror became, "Either you are with us or you are with the terrorists," and the

American slogan became, "Let's roll"—the purported last words of the terrorist-fighting hero, Todd Beamer on United Flight 93 that crashed in Pennsylvania. (4) Manipulated language. To study American propaganda in America's "New War" (CNN's tag line), one must analyze content and symbols and approach events like a political campaign or commercial. The phrase, "War on Terrorism" is itself a propaganda message. By design, it elevates the language of conflict, suggesting that all other options (negotiation, international courts of justice, international policing) have been exhausted, when the reality is that they were never seriously considered. Once war has been declared, it is unlikely that dialogue around roots causes can occur until the war mission has been completed and deemed successful. The Bush administration has assured (perhaps scared) the American people and the world that this "New War" will be a long and drawn-out campaign, not won on the watch of President Bush, suggesting years, if not decades, of fighting. Immediately, the war on terror transforms much of the media coverage into drama and sensation, because wars are fought between enemies who fight to the death and seek little common ground or solutions that require compromise. (5) Nonrational thinking. The message to the American public is to simply define the problem as an attack on freedom, to present a simplified, readily understood case that "terrorist parasites" want to destroy freedom and democracy. To support the case, an effective propagandist wants to make sure that the case includes plenty of omnibus phrases and symbols—American flags, U.S. Armed Forces, and experts who can lead us, like the avuncular Secretary of Defense Donald Rumsfeld, as well as a suddenly popular wartime President. Omnibus words such as "freedom" and "liberty" are the shorthand symbols of the propagandists—they carry vague general meanings that arouse emotions (fear or hate of our enemy, pride in one's own leadership, in our armed forces). These symbols provide a shorthand dictionary for the conflict. So when you are asked why we fight, you can answer quickly and with a moral imperative: "We fight to defend freedom."

James Warburg, deputy director of the U.S. Office of War Information for Europe in World War II, claimed that wartime propaganda is effective only when linked to a national policy that it can exploit and with which the masses of mankind can identify. It is for this reason that the 9/11 attacks were packaged as our generation's Pearl Harbor and the United States invasions and occupations of Afghanistan and Iraq as Operations Defending Democracy, Liberty, and Freedom—all of which evokes positive emotional reactions in majorities of people. This leaves little wiggle room for someone to be *against* the war, because what does being against the war then mean? You *don't* support freedom, liberty, or democracy? President Bush quickly succeeded in defining the parameters of our national dialogue in the war on terrorism when he said, "Either you are against us or you are with us." He wasn't talking just to the terrorist "parasites" but also to the American people. A or B. No C.

"I think this conflict is going to require a suspension of freedom and rights unlike anything we have seen, at least since World War II, " said Marlin Fitzwater, the press secretary to Bush, Sr., in the *New York Times* of October 7, 2001. Against a backdrop of the CBS news anchor and national journalist Dan Rather declaring on David Letterman's show his willingness to do whatever President Bush asks him to do in the war effort, Fitzwater's prediction is not likely to be any cause for alarm in the media–mind war environment.

There are few rewards for people in the United States who dissent from the United States information war. What person puts "citizen activist" or "dissident" on a résumé? You don't meet with the employment recruiter who exclaims with glee, "I see you picketed Enron headquarters over the weekend!" The Bush administration has chosen not to link the proposed doubling of the new Freedom Corps and Peace Corps to true national security goals of fully funded education, job training, community development, and social and economic justice. Right now, the community-service framework is about individual achievement, giving back to society, but not about community organizing that confronts the status quo and concentrated power.

In the United States, you are not likely to hear much discussion of popular organizing outside of the framework of doing what's good to support the war on terrorism.[48] Each year I'm assailed by the politically palatable "I Have a Dream" speech of Martin Luther King, Jr., which focuses on the individual charismatic figure we've come to know and honor. What you never hear rebroadcast is the anti-war speech that King gave at Riverside Church in 1967, in which he said that the United States was "the greatest purveyor of violence in the world today." From Vietnam to South Africa to Latin America, King said, the United States was "on the wrong side of a world revolution." King questioned "our alliance with the landed gentry of Latin America," and asked why the United States was suppressing revolutions "of the shirtless and barefoot people" in the Third World instead of supporting them. In foreign policy, King also offered an economic critique, complaining about "capitalists of the West investing huge sums of money in Asia, Africa and South America, only to take the profits out with no concern for the social betterment of the countries."[49] You won't hear *that* other dream of Martin Luther King because it questions United States policy, this dream would shift the national dialogue from "polite" patter about whether or not we'll invade Iraq to the impolite analysis of United States military arms sales to despotic regimes that suppress democratic development.

According to the unofficial "Dean" of American Journalism, Walter Lippmann, democracy in America is defined as that which allows the specialized class (to use Lippmann's words) to direct public affairs. In *The Phantom Public*, Lippmann said that the public is "a mere phantom. It is an abstraction. The public must be put in its place so that it may exercise its own powers, but no less and perhaps even more, so that each of us may live free of the trampling and roar of a bewildered herd."[50] And so goes America's information war in the twenty-first century.

Why I Write vs. Why We Fight

□ □ □

BILL BENNETT IS THE DIRECTOR of Empower America, one of the wealthiest of the right-wing Washington, D.C. think tanks, whose motto is "ensuring that government actions foster growth, economic well-being, freedom and individual responsibility." Empower America is not your typical inside-the-Beltway think tank that issues annual reports or occasional policy statements known as white papers that go unread on some Congress member's staff assistant's desk. Empower America is a full-frontal assault organization involved in changing national policy through active engagement of public opinion. As cited in its mission statement: "In implementing our free-market, entrepreneurial principles into law, we are convinced, through actual experience, that we are the most effective 'delivery' system in existence." Empower America's board of directors includes former Clinton Defense Secretary William Cohen, Republican vice presidential candidate Jack Kemp, and Reagan's ambassador to the United Nations, Jeane Kirkpatrick. But Bill Bennett serves as Empower America's omnipresent spokesman. Empower America favors a foreign policy that rejects "shortsighted isolationism and imprudent multilateralism," which could be redefined as advocating international intervention whenever the United States unilateral interests are at stake. Bennett, who served as Ronald Reagan's education secretary and

George Bush Sr.'s "drug czar," (under King George?), joined forces with former CIA director James Woolsey in the spring of 2002 to found Americans for Victory over Terrorism (AVOT) as a sort of public relations arm of the Bush war on terrorism. A full-page ($128,000) AVOT advertisement in the March 10, 2002 Sunday edition of the *New York Times* attacked the radical Islam of the twenty-first century as an enemy "no less dangerous and no less determined than the twin menaces of fascism and communism we faced in the 20th century." But AVOT went further by blasting domestic enemies "who are attempting to use this opportunity to promulgate their agenda of 'blame America first.'" In that second flank attack, AVOT aligned with Lynne Cheney (wife of Vice President Dick Cheney), who helped to organize the American Council of Trustees and Alumni (ACTA), whose fall 2001 report, "Defending Civilization: How Our Universities are Failing America," citing blame-America-itis and anti-war bias among hundreds of American professors. The report included 117 critical quotes from university students and professors in the early days after 9/11 to show proof that American universities were the "weak link" in the war on terror.

In April 2002, with thoughts of the war on dissent at the forefront of my mind, I attended a global-policy conference in Los Angeles that featured Bill Bennett as a keynote speaker on charter education reform. Not one to miss out on an impromptu opportunity to meet and greet, I told Mr. Bennett about a letter I had sent to Empower America in 1998, inviting him to be a commencement speaker at New England College where I was then teaching political science. As a college professor who had influence over young people, I supported Bennett's speaking out at that time in support of personal behavior and responsibility and agreed with him that

President Clinton's behavior with Monica Lewinsky in the Oval Office had sullied the office of the American presidency and damaged Clinton's legacy in history. Further, Clinton took advantage of an asymmetrical power relationship over a subordinate, something I'm keenly aware of in the professor/student dynamic. Since some of my students had an "everybody's doing it" attitude toward Bill Clinton's personal behavior in the White House, I thought Bennett might have a refreshing moral lesson to offer young graduates. As it turned out, our commencement fell on Mother's Day and his secretary explained that he never scheduled events on that day so that he could spend it with his mother. (It *is* nice to know he's a Mom loyalist.)

While Bennett was waiting for the elevator at the Beverly Hilton Hotel, I asked him about obtaining a copy of his latest book, *Why We Fight: Moral Clarity and the War on Terrorism*, which I knew addressed public criticism that could hurt the national resolve in the war on terror. Jeffrey Kwitowski, the press secretary for Empower America, pulled out the last copy he had and handed it to me. I promised that I would write a review. He replied, "Great, as long as it's positive."

Jeff, I'll try to be as positive as I can, given the circumstances.

Bennett's title, *Why We Fight*, is borrowed from the famous government propaganda films made by the American film director Frank Capra during World War II. Capra was hired by the U.S. Army Morale Branch under General George C. Marshall and made a Major. The "Why We Fight" film series explained America's entry into World War II to drafted GIs and their families and underscored the country's need for personal sacrifice in wartime. The most famous film in the series, *Prelude to War*, divided the world into forces of light (the United States and the Allied Powers) and darkness (Germany and the Axis Powers). Capra noted that the inspiration for the series came after he watched the Nazi propaganda film *Triumph des Willens* (*Triumph of the Will*) by the German director Leni Riefenstahl, which had "scared the hell out of me."[51] He wanted to make an American propaganda film that would support the American-Allied cause for freedom and democracy.

William Bennett shares Capra's need to support the war cause—in this case, the Bush administration's war on terror. Bennett's Weltanschauung is driven by righteous anger at cultural elites (himself excluded), like writers, university professors, and journalists who dare to question the government at war. These people who question force and war are, in his view, biased and morally deficient:

Why has the critique of violence taken such hold among us, and why does it exercise such influence? The answer is paradoxical. Contrary to the myth of our nation as violence-prone, Americans in fact are a peaceful people, averse to conflict. That is the larger truth about us. Our habits are the habits of a commercial society, resting on rich deposits of social trust and on laws that regulate and protect transactions of every kind. Our outlook is the outlook of a democratic polity, guided by the spirit of accommodation and compromise, superintended by guarantees of due process and judicial review.[52]

William Bennett's book exemplifies a series of efforts under way to scare American citizens into self-censorship. University professors remain easy targets for allegedly causing their students to hate the United States by raising questions about the motives and policies of the government. To Bennett, declarations of war seem to imply cessation of critical thinking, especially on college campuses:

> In short, many in the "peace party" who cloak their arguments in moral objections to war are really expressing their hostility to America, and it does the cause of clarity no good to pretend otherwise. That hostility—in more than a few cases, hatred is a more accurate word—is many-sided and has a long history, and we shall be encountering facets of it in our discussion. But where armed conflict is concerned, the arguments of today's "peace party" are basically rooted in the period of the Vietnam War and its aftermath. It was then that the critique of the United States as an imperialist or 'colonialist' power, wreaking its evil will on the hapless peoples of the third world, became a kind of slogan on the Left. This same critique would, in due course, find a home in certain precincts of the Democratic party, and in more diluted form, would inform the policy preferences of the Carter and Clinton administrations, and it is with us still. It is especially prevalent in our institutions of higher learning.[53]

If you follow Bennett's logic, then America as a country worth fighting for must include a fight that is absolutist in language, thought, and action. If you don't absolutely defend your country, right or wrong, the logical fallacy goes, then you give aid and comfort to the enemy. It is this condemnation of those who dare to question, the simplification of complex issues into either/or categories, and Bennett's attacks on what he calls the "peace party" that exposes the shades of gray that make me recommend a reading of *Why We Fight* for clarity in consciousness. In the end, a positive review!

Opinion Control on the Next War

FREEDOM TO FEAR, FREEDOM FROM THINKING

*For a prince must have two kinds of fear: one internal as
regards his subjects, one external as regards foreign powers.*
—NICCOLO MACHIAVELLI, THE PRINCE

☐ ☐ ☐

AMERICA IS A NATION IN AN information war with itself. On the
one hand, American journalists and editors tout the virtues of
free and open media, the international imperative for the free
flow of information, and the constitutional responsibility for
government to avoid dominating the flow and exchange of
information. On the other hand, these free-media principles
have been wanting throughout the United States invasions
and occupations of Afghanistan and Iraq. Analysis of the
media coverage of the war with Iraq offers an interesting case
study of modern information and opinion management. To
learn more, we need to look back briefly to the last war with
Iraq under a different Bush administration to see how the son
responds to the father's example. There is plenty of evidence
to suggest that familial history repeats.

"In retrospect and in balance, the remarkable control of
American consciousness during and after the war must be
regarded as a signal achievement of mind management, perhaps even more impressive than the rapid military victory."[54]
Herbert I. Schiller wrote these words in May 1991 for the

French newspaper, *Le Monde Diplomatique*, to explain the first Bush administration's great success in controlling information about the war and American press acquiescence in withholding information that the public needed in order to make a sound decision about critical issues of war and peace. It wasn't until after the Persian Gulf War that the www.udesen.com press claimed any complicity in its reportage, as when Tom Wicker of the *New York Times* reported "the real and dangerous point is that the Bush administration and the military were so successful in controlling information about the war they were able to tell the public just about what they wanted the public to know. Perhaps worse, press and public, largely acquiesced in the disclosure of only selected information."[55] That public acquiescence followed from the American people's habits of media consumption. As Michael Deaver, spin doctor to President Reagan, gloated in the *New York Times*, "Television is where 80% of the people get their information," and what was done to control that information in the six weeks of war "couldn't [have] been better."[56]

A March–April 1991 *Columbia Journalism Review* (March–April 1991) survey of Gulf War coverage noted how much information about domestic dissent against the war was kept off those television screens. As pointed out by the consumer advocate and subsequent Green Party presidential candidate Ralph Nader in the article, the January 26, 1991, peace march in Washington, D.C. was "probably the biggest citizen demonstration ever...in winter," but CBS gave it a four-second mention.[57] Similarly, a senior House Democrat, Henry Gonzales of Texas, who chaired the House Banking Committee, sponsored a resolution to impeach President Bush on the war in Iraq, but this action went unreported in the broadcast media. Bob Sipschen, *Newsweek* correspondent in the Gulf, wrote in the *Los Angeles Times* March 1991 that

"Desert Storm was really two wars: The Allies against the Iraqis and the military against the press. I had more guns pointed at me by Americans and Saudis who were into controlling the press than in all my years of actual combat."[58]

One could argue that the military control of American media in Gulf War I was not always necessary given the self-censorship of the American press, particularly regarding the coverage of foreign opinion. Much of the global opposition to the military invasion of Iraq came to light weeks after the war's end. A paid advertisement in the March 18, 1991, *New York Times* sponsored by a private group of concerned Japanese citizens illustrated how widely opposed the Japanese people had been to the use of military force in Iraq. "When the Japanese Government tried to send our already unconstitutional Self-Defense Forces to the Gulf, rallies, meetings, and demonstrations were held all over the country." Spain in 1991 was like the Spain of 2003, another center of massive public opposition to war and its government's contribution to the Allied effort in Iraq, but these opinions received no media attention. Even when such a situation was covered, a four-second flash of national demonstrations in North Africa was no balance to a widely distributed image of Egyptian President Mubarak endorsing the United States' policy. "What was repeated endlessly for domestic consumption [in the U.S. media] was that the United States was engaged in an allied effort, supported by the United Nations, that also embraced the sentiments of a good part of the world," wrote Schiller in *Le Monde Diplomatique* (May 1991).

The United States media were as utterly unconcerned with Iraqi casualties in 1991 as they would later be unconcerned with Afghan citizen casualties in fall 2001 and again with Iraqi casualties in 2003. When asked in March 1991 about the number of Iraqi dead from United States air and land operations, then General Colin Powell stated, "It's really not a number I'm terribly interested in."[59] A noted exception to typical press coverage was the reporting of the bombing of the Baghdad shelter in February 1991 that killed hundreds of Iraqi families, an event that had to be reported because it was happening live and could not be ignored. But even then, the Pentagon was ready to explain that the shelter was a deliberate attempt by Hussein to win a propaganda advantage in the war by stirring up sympathy for innocent victims. CNN's round-the-clock, on-site reporting to a global audience of viewers made the event a legend. But the coverage's of exclusion of dissident voices and anything critical of the dominant position on the war was not that much different from stateside network coverage. Nevertheless, by the end of the 1991 war in Iraq, a Los Angeles–sponsored poll "discovered that two institutions enjoyed significant boosts from the war—the military and the television news organizations. Seventy-three percent of Americans felt that television reporters dug harder into the war than their print competitors."[60] In the same issue of the newspaper, President "George Bush said that the press kept its eyes and ears open during the war."[61]

Similarly, television coverage on Iraq from August 2002 to March 2003 was overwhelmingly dominated by the image of a resolute Commander-in-Chief Bush and his closest advisers who stuck to one dominant view—that Saddam must go. In the months leading up to the first anniversary of 9/11, President Bush merged the case for attacking Iraq into the ongoing war on terror, thereby cinching any dissent. By cleverly linking the perpetual fear of shadowy terrorist groups to the leftover problem of Saddam Hussein in Iraq, the American people had no political option but to join the bandwagon of support for the President on Iraq, given the only alternative offered of support for terrorists. To quote Bill Maher, deposed late-night host of *Politically Incorrect*, on the state of free speech in America: "When you ride alone, you ride with Bin Laden."

With such tools as the USA PATRIOT Act, the Bush Doctrine that arose from the ashes of 9/11 successfully broadened the rhetorical "war on terror" from those international terrorist groups like Al Qaeda that were potentially linked to the 9/11 attacks into a perpetual war that extends to "criminal investigations that have little or no connection to terrorism."[62] In three separate speeches to military academies (The Citadel, Virginia Military Institute, and West Point) that were not critically analyzed by the United States media, Bush told his enthusiastic listeners that Afghanistan was just the beginning of a long campaign to change government leadership. In his June 1, 2002, graduation speech at West Point, Bush outlined his Newthink war doctrine that emphasized action over reaction:

> For much of the last century, America's defense relied on the Cold War doctrines of deterrence and containment … new threats also require new thinking. Deterrence—the promise of massive retaliation against nations—means nothing against shadowy terrorist networks with no nation or citizens to defend. Containment is not possible when unbalanced dictators with weapons of mass destruction can deliver those weapons on missiles or secretly provide them to terrorist allies… the war on terror will not be won on the defensive. We must take the battle to the enemy, disrupt his plans, and confront the worst threats before they emerge. In the world we have entered, the only path to safety is the path of action. And this nation will act.[63]

The phrase, "war on terror," Nicholas Lemann of *The New Yorker* wrote, "has entered the language so fully, and framed the way people think about how the United States is reacting to the September 11 attacks so completely, that the idea that declaring and waging war on terror was not the sole, inevitable, logical consequence of the attacks just isn't in circulation."[64]

The greatest gift of British writer George Orwell was to present the ways political leaders often control language for their own ends. In his 1946 essay, "Politics and the English Language," he argued that language should express and not conceal thought. However, "in our time, political speech and writing are largely the defense of the indefensible. Political language "is designed to make lies sound truthful and murder respectable, and to give an appearance of solidity to pure wind."[65] Orwell's classic example of language control is the slogan, "war is peace." Lest we think that it's impossible to hold two opposing ideas in our minds at the same time and actually believe in them, think about the language that defines our present situation with Iraq. When Bush said, "We're at war" upon hearing that a second plane had flown into the World Trade Center, many of us may have thought then that war meant something with a definite conclusion, like World War I or World War II. Yet the slogan, "war on terror," is a symbol of perpetual thinking about perpetual war. Its sister slogan, "Either you are with us, or you are with the terrorists," symbolizes the triumph of one accepted mode of thought, controlled thought, over any other modes of thought (free thought, dissenting thought) that might actually challenge the position of the state and its leaders.

By the time of the October 2002 Congressional vote on attacking Iraq, there was really only one acceptable position on the issue using the accepted linguistic metaphor, war on terror. With no Democratic opposition and minimal press coverage of anti-war opposition, Bush was free to utter statements like the one he made in his radio address to the nation on October 12, 2002: "America is speaking with one voice."[66] With the Republican majority takeover in the November 5 elections, Bush was riding in the saddle of the imperial president, a picture of resolute firmness and almost eager willingness to engage in perpetual war against "those who hate freedom," another favored phrase that chills any serious debate about issues of life and death.

In late November 2002, the legendary investigative journalist and Watergate hero Bob Woodward helped further the cause of unquestioning thought about Iraq when he took over America's television screens to discuss his book, *Bush at War*, a yearlong portrait of the President. While perspectives from anti-war activists both here and abroad remained almost invisible in America's broadcast media, and their proponents were left to talk amongst themselves in the dissident print press and on the Web,[67] there was Woodward seemingly everywhere on television (CNN, *60 Minutes*) touting the virtues of the prince—er, president. Woodward reassured the American people that Bush the son had no problem, like his father, with "the vision thing." In fact, this president was absolutely sure of himself and, according to Woodward, knew exactly how his presidency would define itself in the shadow of 9/11. The picture that emerged was of a president whose personality triumphed, to manage public opinion to the point of unanimity (one voice).

Consider this transcript of an exchange on CNN's *Larry King Live* program between a caller and Woodward about regarding former U.N. Inspector Scott Ritter. Ritter, a Republican who for months drew large crowds on college campuses, and was interviewed in alternative media as well as the *New York Times* about his outspoken denunciation of the war against Iraq. Ritter's steady questioning of the motivations for war is contrasted to the "simple" lesson of September 11—that threats must be taken care of early—proffered by President Bush's national security adviser, Condoleezza Rice:

> CALLER: Yes, good evening, gentlemen. I recently observed a lecture being given by a gentleman who was a previous Iraqi arms inspector. He was also, I believe, a Gulf War combat veteran, a man by the name of Scott Ritter. And I'm most interested in what Mr. Woodward's opinion would be of Mr. Ritter's credibility and his message.

> WOODWARD: There's an immense amount of skepticism. I understand Scott Ritter feels very, very strongly about that. I've talked to people who know about the intelligence and the information we have. And there is no question that there is something there. There also is no question that Saddam Hussein is kind of an industrial strength package of psychiatric disorders and a very dangerous man. Now, whether you have to go to war to solve the problem remains to be seen, but he is a threat and one of the things Condi Rice said on the record when I talked to her about this, said the lesson of September 11 is simple. Take care of threats early. Not late. That's what should have been done with Bin Laden and there is a feeling about Saddam on this now. We'll see how it plays out. Scott Ritter, I don't know enough about him. I'm sorry, sir.[68]

The dissent and questioning of an experienced veteran and official is simply dismissed, while the supposedly "simple" solution of war is repeated. However the war on terror spreads and evolves at home and abroad, the information war will continue to be led by the control of language from the top. In the case of Iraq, slogans and facile statements of freedom over tyranny from the President seem to satisfy the appetite of the press, while opposing thought from the grassroots requires evidence beyond reasonable doubt. Is the lesson of September 11 as simple as this President would have us believe? Why do we as a nation continue to acquiesce in support of an administration that gets away with simplifying very complex situations of life and death? In part, the situation is due to instant bestsellers like Woodward's *Bush at War* that promote individual personality over the social context. He could have written *America at War*, a sort of people's history of life after 9/11, but that would have required more than a two-hour one-on-one with the President at his ranch in Crawford, Texas. More important, Jacques Ellul writes in *Propaganda*, there can be no unanimity of thought without the steady propaganda of a political chief, "in whom everyone finds himself, in whom everyone hopes and projects himself, and for whom everything is possible and permissible."[69]

The President's pet slogan, "war on terrorism" remains a convenient state tactic to control public opinion, expand the climate of fear, and shut down opposition to war in Iraq and elsewhere. Many peace and social-change activists in the United States and elsewhere are legitimately concerned with the manner in which countering terrorism through better intelligence and policing has been replaced by aggressive war talk about "preemptive strikes" and "regime change." To many, we live in a climate of fear that chills dissent from the nation's declaration of war. But as Lt. General William Odom

(Ret.) U.S. Army said on C-SPAN's *Washington Journal*: "Terrorism is not an enemy. It cannot be defeated. It's a tactic. It's about as sensible to say we declare war on night attacks and expect we're going to win that war. We're not going to win the war on terrorism. And it does whip up fear. Acts of terror have never brought down liberal democracies. Acts of parliament have closed a few."[70]

If, as General Odom states, terrorism can never be defeated, the nation's advantage in declaring a perpetual war on terrorism is to stymie creative thinking about alternatives. The purpose of such propaganda phrases as "war on terrorism" and attacking "those who hate freedom" is to paralyze individual thought as well as to condition people to act as one mass, as when President Bush attempted to end debate on Iraq by claiming that the American people were of one voice. The modern war president removes the individual nature of those who live in it by forcing us into a uniform state where the complexities of those we fight are erased. The enemy—terrorism, Iraq, Bin Laden, Hussein—becomes one threatening category, something to be defeated and destroyed, so that the public response will be one of reaction to fear and threat rather than creatively and independently thinking for oneself.

Our best hope for overcoming perpetual thinking about war and perpetual fear about both real and imagined threats is to question our leaders and their use of empty slogans that offer little rationale, explanation or historical context. Lessons of 9/11 are not as simple or as black-and-white as presented by President Bush. I do not believe that a nation of 270 million has collectively decided that we must go defeat threats whenever and wherever, because it is neither possible to do so everywhere given our limited resources, and as the missing weapons of mass destruction in Iraq exemplify, we can never be sure that the threats that require military intervention are even real. Further, threats of terror are much more amorphous than the real threats to economic and social security we are experiencing. Is a nation without a national healthcare package a threat to its public safety and security? Yes, but this Administration is not utilizing the same energy to defeat our self-made threats as it is to defeating those foreign enemies that threaten our domestic tranquility. The triumph of absolutist rhetoric like terror and freedom or good and evil impedes our ability to distinguish real threats, which must be combatted and controlled, from self-serving threats that reinforce state power and control over public freedom. Nevertheless, we cannot blame President Bush or the press for our own lack of initiative in organizing ongoing resistance to such power and control. Democracy demands constant vigilance.

Sister Soldya

CHARLOTTE BEERS AND THE MOTHER OF ALL MARKETING CAMPAIGNS

☐ ☐ ☐

THROUGH HER TENURE (1992–1997) at Ogilvy & Mather, Charlotte Beers was best known for her core credo of "brand stewardship," otherwise known as the art of creating, building, and energizing profitable brands, from fast food (KFC) to computers (IBM). Beers wanted the agency to take emotional ownership of the brand through the creation of a brand audit that explored the relationship between the product and the consumer. Questions were asked like, "How does the brand make you *feel* about yourself?" A quintessential Beers moment came when she tossed her car keys on the table at a meeting with Jaguar executives to explore the emotional relationship between a car owner and her car brand. The commercial made from the pitch featured the 1961 Etta James recording, "At last my love has come along, my lonely days are over," playing over the visual of a very satisfied-looking woman driving her Jag. The *Financial Times* of London noted in 1999 that Beers had three obsessions, "brands, brands, brands," and that she "never stops talking about them."[71] This quality may explain why Colin Powell brought Charlotte Beers out of retirement— it was her brand mastery and her ability to make a convincing pitch for Uncle Sam. In a statement before the House Budget Committee in March 2001 following his nomination as Secretary of State, Powell promised, "I'm going to be bringing in people into the public diplomacy function of the department who are going to change from just selling us in the old USIA way to really branding foreign policy, branding the department, marketing the department, marketing American values to the world and not just putting out pamphlets."[72] When Powell, who had first met Beers in the 1990s when both served on the board for Gulfstream Aerospace, nominated Beers as public diplomacy undersecretary, *Advertising Age* reported the nomination the following way: "The State Department, which implemented the Monroe Doctrine, is about to embrace a new doctrine: Branding."

Of her new job, Beers said, "This is the most sophisticated brand assignment that I have ever had."[73] At her Senate confirmation hearing, she promised to infuse all her branding campaigns with emotions: "I'm looking for opportunities to put the legitimate emotional context of who the American people are and their messages in all channels of distribution." From October 2001 until her resignation in March 2003, her creations included pamphlets, brochures, and a four-minute video version of the attacks on the World Trade Center and Pentagon distributed to Ad Council–produced public-service announcements in the United States and abroad, that distilled the Bush administration's version of United States' values and virtues. A State Department Web site targeted at foreigners featured a section on "Muslim Life in America," with pictures of American mosques and smiling American Muslim families. Her efforts were augmented by appearances of Bush administration officials on the Arabic TV network, Al-Jazeera, to explain the United States' bombing campaign in Afghanistan, as well as House legislation to establish Radio Free Afghanistan and a new radio service for the Middle East targeted at an atypical Voice of America listener: an Arab male, twenty-five years of age or younger.

Charlotte Beers was sworn into office as Under Secretary of State for Public Diplomacy and Public Affairs just three weeks to the day after the terror attacks on the United States. Despite a lack of experience in politics or public diplomacy, Beers came from the highest pedigree in advertising—the only executive to serve as Chairman and CEO of J. Walter Thompson Worldwide and Ogilvy & Mather, two of the top ten global advertising agencies. Known as the Steel Magnolia of Advertising for her ability to combine a feminine Texas charm with the forthright determination to break the glass ceiling all the way to the top, Beers was immediately thrust into the media spotlight as head of the administration's new mind war on terrorism.

It was clear that shifting the spotlight from behind-the-scenes product guru to front-and-center government propaganda CEO was more than Beers might have bargained for with the appointment, despite Colin Powell's defense of her before members of Congress: "Guess what? She got *me* to buy Uncle Ben's rice. So there is nothing wrong with getting somebody who knows how to sell something." Media wags had a field day with the obvious avuncular comparisons. Some reporters began to weigh in just how the first female product manager for Uncle Ben's Rice could manage the mother of all marketing campaigns—branding Uncle Sam. The *Washington Post* reported, "She's been pilloried by pundits on at least two continents, who've mocked the whole idea of advertising America."[74] Andrew Alexander of the *Daily Mail* of London wrote, "One shouldn't laugh, really, but I must confess to a short guffaw on reading that Washington's new war propaganda chief is a woman head of an advertising agency whose personal triumphs included Uncle Ben's Rice and Head & Shoulders shampoo."[75] The columnist Frank Rich of the *New York Times* wrote, "The Bush appointee in charge of the propaganda effort is a C.E.O. (from Madison Avenue) chosen not for her expertise in policy or politics but for her salesmanship on behalf of domestic products like Head & Shoulders shampoo. If we can't effectively fight anthrax, I guess it's reassuring to know we can always win the war on dandruff."[76] Steve Lopez of the *Los Angeles Times,* wrote that the White House decision to choose Beers as chief propaganda queen led to his "second out-of-body experience" since the war in Afghanistan had begun on October 7, 2001. (His first out-of-body experience was the White House decision to go with the working title Operation Infinite Justice, which was quickly dumped for the more modest Operation Enduring Freedom.) He seemed befuddled as to why would the White House put an ad executive in charge of America's image war but then sarcastically snipped, "Who knows? Maybe they're onto something. Just the other day I took a sip of Coke and began singing, 'I'd like to teach the world to sing in perfect harmony.' How could anyone hate a nation of peace-loving simpletons for whom the best part of waking up is Folger's in your cup?"[77]

The key question, sarcastic or not, that Lopez and other reporters raised repeatedly in the fall of 2001 was this: Is it possible to sell Uncle Sam the way you sell Uncle Ben? As one who had worked in the United States Information Agency (USIA), which had preceded the Bureau of Public Affairs at the State Department, I didn't think that it would be so simple to construct a battle plan for an image war based solely on a background in product development. Or at least I was hoping that a rebranding strategy wouldn't be seen in marketing terms alone. The United States, at its heart, was an ideal more than a product for sale. But having Beers in charge—a person with zero experience in international politics—seemed to ensure that the branding-America campaign wouldn't even begin to address the fundamental image problems of the United States. The United States image problem stems in part from the perception that our foreign policy is a form of propaganda constructed by and for American corporations; that the McWorld constructed by corporate big business benefits wealthy Westerners at the expense of the world's poor. The American propaganda machine doesn't represent Americans individually. It depicts the most heterogeneous country in the world as a single-minded monolith, and it hasn't begun to tell the story of who and what we are. If the administration was not willing to revamp its foreign policy from which many of the image problems originate, then why not take its public-relations campaign to the streets and neighborhoods of America and out of the corporate corridors of Madison Avenue? Madison Avenue and Washington could explore ways to partner with new or existing nongovernmental organizations (NGOs), such as a citizens' diplomacy corps where teachers, students, and cultural mediators would tell stories about America's strengths in principles and ideals, admit our past mistakes, and broaden our understanding of other histories and cultures. Such an effort would evoke the sentiment expressed by Senator J. William Fulbright, who wrote the Fulbright-Hays Act of 1946 that established the largest post–World War II government-sponsored educational exchange program: "My question is whether America can close the gap between her capacity and her performance. My hope and my belief are that she can, that she has the human resources to conduct her affairs with a maturity which few if any great nations have ever achieved: to be confident but also tolerant, to be rich but also generous, to be willing to teach but also to learn, to be powerful but also wise."[78]

Fulbright's educational and statesmanlike vision for America seems in marked contrast to the all-business branding America campaign spearheaded by someone known at one time as "the most powerful woman in the ad business."[79] Like it or not, an ad woman was in charge of public diplomacy at the State Department, and she was going to work with what she know best. In an exclusive interview with Diane Sawyer, the anchor of *Good Morning America* (where Beers had been a contributor), Sawyer introduced Beers as "the woman whose job it is to tell the world who America is and make the Muslim world understand. Talk about a daunting assignment."[80] Beers acknowledged that reaching the young Arab men taking to the streets to denounce the United States "is one target market that is the most entrenched. And when we do consumer research, which we finally started doing—in a modern marketing way, we learned that they need to believe that Bin Laden is a holy man....But some of the people will not join us at all, but there are many more people in the whole Muslim world who are very vulnerable to this kind of information." Sawyer, taking her cue from the cacophony of voices in opposition to a Madison Avenue ad maven in charge of cultural diplomacy, asked Beers to comment about her detractors. She said, "As you know, some of the Washington establishment sniffed mightily when you arrived, saying several things. First of all, an ad executive coming to do diplomacy. Second of all, saying you cannot sell America like Coca-Cola...Do you want to answer them who say we can't sell it [(America)] the way we sell from Madison Avenue?" Beers replied, "What we are doing is using modern marketing techniques, and we already have one of the world's most sophisticated Web sites and computer facilities in the State Department. When we talk to embassies and—and markets around the world, we desperately need to do a better job of getting communication beyond the elites and the government figures into the mass markets. It's also crucial that we learn how to use emotion in our communication. Al Jazeera lives on emotion and drama and we're content to let everything happen in a logical fashion. This is not a reasonable dialogue we're engaged in; it includes some emotion."

That last statement by Beers may have been a reference to the bureaucratic tendency in the USIA and the State Department to "let the facts speak for themselves" and downplay the important emotional and very human connection necessary for influencing public audiences overseas, but it also implied a cultural stereotype that Arab and Muslim "target markets" are more emotional by nature to begin with and that therefore, if the United States government is seeking greater influence, it must utilize the vernacular nuances that reach people. A better comment would have stressed mutual dialogue, both emotional (heart) and rational (head), that emphasized the need for nations to come together in a shared need to eradicate misunderstandings and misperceptions that incite terrorism and war. Her statement was more homeland than common ground.

During the interview with Diane Sawyer, Beers introduced a radio advertisement associated with the State Department Rewards for Justice program, designed to get Americans to spot terrorists in their midst: "Do you know a terrorist? Not long ago, this would have seemed like a ridiculous question. But not anymore. The United States government is offering rewards up to $25 million for information that prevents an international terrorist act against U.S. persons or property or brings to justice persons who have committed one."[81] The Rewards for Justice print ad showed a picture of September 11 ringleader Mohamed Atta along with the text: "He was spotted in Hamburg, Prague, Florida, Maine. And if someone called us, his picture wouldn't be spotted in this ad, it would have been prevented." The Rewards for Justice Web site included ads targeted specifically at American women. "You, as a woman and perhaps a mother, may be in a unique position to act against international terrorism," states the print ad headlined, "Can a Woman Stop Terrorism?" Beers explained to Sawyer, "I really believe that women do understand and see more in many ways," not mentioning the marketing axiom that women purchase or see more through the purchase of 80 percent of all consumer goods and so are the primary audience of advertisers.

The Rewards for Justice campaign was the most ambitious undertaking in Charlotte Beer's tenure. It was not a Beers brainchild but an expansion of an existing program that began under Reagan in 1984 and had already paid out more than $7 million to twenty-two informants in the United States and abroad before 9/11. She was helped in her effort by Scott Case, a cofounder of Priceline.com, who used his marketing and Internet prowess to set up a private fund for the Rewards for Justice campaign, including "United We Stand" license plates in Florida and other states to subsidize the State Department's reward funds. "This is fighting terrorism with capitalism," Case remarked. "We expect a tsunami of people coming forward with information," as if anticipating a greater turnout of terrorist spotters in a recession.[82] At a news conference for the foreign press in November 2001, Beers unveiled her new campaign. "First we will have print and radio. We are going to follow very soon with banner ads that tap into adjacent Web sites. We will have movie theater clips and maybe even matchbook covers." One reporter asked, "How confident are you that your new campaign is not going to end up like, you know, New Coke or the Edsel?" Against a background of a few cynical reporters' chuckles, he added, "Is there a poster child—a poster man or woman—that you envision to be set up to, you know, represent a symbol of America abroad?" To the first, she responded, "I did a Harvard case study on what happened to

New Coke and if you'll pull it up and read it, you'll get your answer to that." To the second, she said, "Well, you know, in a way, our poster people are President Bush and Secretary Powell, who I think are pretty inspiring symbols of the brand 'The United States.'" That answer got the *Washington Post* reporter Peter Carlson to say, "Brilliant! Asked to suggest a symbol of America, she immediately named her boss and her boss's boss. It was a rare demonstration of the kind of talent that can take a person to the very heights of the advertising business—or the federal government."[83]

Beers believed that the essential elements of marketing the United States brand were not unlike those she marketed throughout her Madison Avenue career. In an interview with *Business Week*, she explained that with a hostile target market, "We are going to have to deliver the intangible assets of the United States, things like our belief system and values. This calls up a different set of skills...much closer to the kind of disciplines we always had to have in advertising."[84] And the U.S.A. brand, like with any great brand, "the leverageable asset is the emotional underpinning of the brand—or what people believe, what they think, how they feel when they use it. I am much more comfortable with that dimension of the assignment, because I've dealt with it before." What's different this time? Dialogue. Beers admits. "Countries like the United States, which are big and powerful, will always translate into arrogance if there is no dialogue." (She was most "on target" with that statement.) Beers and her staff consulted with a list of at least four hundred American Muslims, fielded traditional consumer research in Jordan, Lebanon, and other Middle Eastern countries, and called upon a kitchen cabinet of corporate marketing whizzes from the nonprofit Advertising Council to private research and marketing firms. Their global marketing research was nonpolicy wonkish by design. Beers noted that "The government is well poised to give you research in terms of major policy issues, but they're not going to tell you much about what will help you talk to a four-teen-year-old boy who has been inculcated for years with a really different vantage point." To start with, the premise was different from just explaining foreign-policy positions, as wonks were trained to do. As Allen Rosenshine, chairman of BBDO Worldwide, remarked about the USA rebranding cam-paign, "We have to start from the basis of 'OK, people hate us.' If all we do is go out and tell them America is the land of the free and the home of the brave, we're damn fools."[85]

The problem with the Rewards for Justice program was that it tapped into a post-9/11 American awareness that a ter-rorist was hiding behind every tree. It harkened back to the Advertising Council's "Loose Lips Sink Ships" crusade of the 1940s that warned Americans not to spill secrets to the enemy living among us. As Beers told reporters at the mar-keting rollout for RFJ, "This might have been unthinkable before September eleventh, but this is the first time we real-ized that we must ask every citizen in the United States to think about information they might have, because for the first time we know clearly terrorists are here. They have been here among us, and they are here."[86]

A basic program that emphasized mental alertness about suspicious behavior is one thing, but what kind of information would it invite? Would a Middle Eastern–looking man or someone who just looks Arab merit a tip to the Rewards for Justice hotline? The program ran the risk of becoming, inad-vertently or not, a collection center of data for people who were guilty of being associated through religion or ethnicity with the attackers of September 11. As Jim Zogby of the Arab American Institute in Washington, D.C., warned, the State Department ad campaign might turn into a citizens' watch hunt gone astray. Better to beef up intelligence work than to encourage neighbors to turn in neighbors.

The Rewards for Justice advertising campaign corresponded to a rise in advertising as propaganda following September 11. While advertisers gave a brief reprieve to the American psyche in the first few weeks after 9/11, very shortly the Big Three automakers in Detroit were compelling Americans to do their patriotic duty and get back to the American road with big American SUVs and trucks. The rush to glorify the pleasures of capitalist materialism in the face of fear and uncertainty helped to soothe the troubled psyche that all was not good on Main Street, U.S.A., and reminded the individual consumer that the socioeconomic system was still working just fine. As if to further reinforce in surround sound what this system was really all about, the Advertising Council initiated its own Campaign for Freedom to remind Americans just how good we have it—pass it on. Presented as an unprecedented volunteer effort from the advertising industry to assist Americans during the war on terrorism (as if we'd asked for "Ad" Nauseam), the Freedom PSAs celebrated American freedom in the face of terror. All of the TV and print ads appeared with the tag line, "Freedom. Appreciate it. Cherish it. Protect it." The campaign was inspired by President Bush's declaration on September 11 that American freedom itself was attacked on 9/11, and so Americans must vigilantly defend freedom (probably through military force) wherever and whenever it comes under future threat or attack. In his book *The Uneasy Persuasion*, Michael Schudson states that advertising in a capitalist system like the United States serves basically the same function as the state-sanctioned socialist realist art of the Soviet Union. "American advertising, like socialist realist art, simplifies and typifies. It does not claim to picture reality as it should be."[87]

One Campaign for Freedom Ad included the following text of its own advertising version of reality: "Because while rights like freedom of speech, freedom of religion and freedom of the press get all the attention in the Constitution, the smaller liberties you can enjoy everyday in America are no less important or worthy of celebration. Your right to backyard barbeques, sleeping in on Sunday and listening to any darned music you please can be just as fulfilling as your right to vote for the president. Maybe even more so because you can enjoy these freedoms personally and often."[88] Such ad copy simplifies and typifies the level of intellectual rigor that arose from the ashes of 9/11.

The question remains of whether it is necessary to rebrand the United States. To many throughout the world, America is already a brand, a multitrillion-dollar brand of mass consumerism, cultural and military dominance, led by such worldwide symbols as Marlboro, McDonald's, Boeing, Coca-Cola, and General Electric. The selling of America, even in a new format or packaging, may add to the global perception that continues to plague the United States. America, Inc.™ is presented in glittering generalities of good freedom and democracy fighting evil tyranny and fanaticism the world over, but our global audience knows that the reality of America is quite different from the rhetoric. Despite all the branding, to many the United States is seen as a violent international aggressor with a military doctrine of open preemptive strike, the world's leader in arms trafficking and economic globalization, an aggressive opponent of the International Criminal Court and anti–global warming treaties, and a staunch supporter of Israel throughout its brutal military occupation and collective punishment of Palestinians. For these reasons, and as long as United States international interventions favors military solutions over humanitarian assistance, many parts of the world will continue to be receptive to the kind of anti–United States sentiment and rhetoric of groups like the Taliban and Al Qaeda.

Branding America is certainly not the best strategy for ending terrorism. As a superpower, the United States is very used to doing the talking and marketing of its position on the global stage. The time has come for the United States to listen more to the legitimate grievances that even our allies have with the unilateral position the United States takes in so many geopolitical arenas. Likewise, in culture and communication, the United States supports a free flow of information in theory but not in practice, preferring to let the market, and not governments, determine that flow.

Charlotte Beers' brand-first approach to public diplomacy after 9/11 parallels an overall decline in affection toward United States brands overseas. The rising tide of anti-Americanism, in part the result of the invasions and occupations of Afghanistan and Iraq, now seems to be hurting the image of American multinationals. A 2003 survey by RoperASW saw a connection for the first time in its five-year history of such polling "when a survey of 30,000 consumers in 30 major economies found that those who felt an increasing alienation from American culture were also likely to report a growing disinclination to eat at McDonald's or to buy Nike shoes."[89] In Germany, a traditional post–World War II ally that became a hotbed of protest against the United States war with Iraq, the shift in brand power was dramatic: the number of consumers who claimed that they regularly use Nike products fell from 49 percent in 2002 to 29 percent in 2003, while the number who said they regularly eat at McDonald's fell from 43 to 34 percent in the same span. Further, the survey uncovered falling or stagnant scores in 11 out of 12 top American multinationals' "brand power," a measure of how well top companies are known and liked. In contrast, nine out of 12 top European and Asian multinationals saw their scores rise.

What we might want to do is to take a step back from our obvious historical advantage in marketing and advertising and think about how we might build bridges toward mutual understanding between the people of the United States and people of other countries. Our dominant ability to huckster our image overseas is what fuels misperceptions and feeds stereotypes to the effect that the United States cares most about market share and least about sharing. The world continues to view us predominantly as a product, not as a country of diverse peoples with dissenting positions. Trying to tell America's story to the world through means to illustrate concepts of freedom, civil liberties, justice, and pluralism is a necessary chapter but not the entire book. Madison Avenue, Hollywood, and the White House must do their triad campaign, but their storytelling will always be somewhat suspect as manufactured spin that tilts in favor of a particular United States policy or product tie-in. What is still needed is a public campaign to tell America's story to the world—from Rewards for Justice to Rewards for Dialogue directed by the American people and their overseas neighbors. This project should be as authentic as possible, not driven by merchandising, branding, or buying. Its tag line could be, "Let's listen and learn for our own sake." Globally-oriented newspapers like the *Christian Science Monitor* and the *International Herald Tribune* could devote a weekly section to this Global Dialogue Project, inviting citizens across the globe to tell stories about their lives—how they live, what they desire for their children, what they wish to know about how people live in other countries. It's a small leap from the self-help advice of Dear Abby to the global knowledge database of Dear Global

Citizen. An influx of a few millions could sponsor more surveys along the lines of the Pew Center's Global Attitudes Survey to poll citizens both here and abroad on our impressions of each other and the nations in which we live.

September 11 has forced American citizens to look within ourselves as a global people. Preventing people from committing desperate terrorist attacks is as much, if not more, about overcoming cultural mindsets that set us apart from each other out of fear and ignorance. It is not about celebrating the freedom of the American barbeque. The post–September 11 era means that no country is isolated from the realities of any other. In a split second, in the most horrific way, we became Marshall McLuhan's global village. However critical I am of Ms. Beers' path to market Uncle Sam, it must be said to her credit that she did bring greater public awareness to the critical importance of American public diplomacy in preventing terrorism. Now is the greatest opportunity to come together—not through Charlotte Beer's legacy of the bottom line or the merchandising aisle—but through our open hearts and learning minds and through a real willingness to reassess and change our own policies at home and abroad.

The Last Three Feet

The really crucial link in the international communications chain is the last three feet, which is best bridged by personal contact—one person talking to another.
—EDWARD R. MURROW, USIA DIRECTOR 1961–1963

□ □ □

HOW IRONIC THAT A BROADCAST giant like Ed Murrow would value personal contact over mass media to change foreign attitudes and influence behavior. Perhaps Murrow's "This...Is London" radio broadcasts during the air raids of World War II convinced him that it's better to conduct international diplomacy on the front end of conflict rather than after the crash landing. When President Kennedy appointed the legendary journalist to head America's propaganda agency, USIA, in 1961, Murrow promised that under his watch, the agency would "operate on the basis of truth...we report events in context; we explain why things happen. But we do not lie, we do not cheat, we do not suppress—and as a result, we are able to achieve a high degree of believability and persuasiveness."[90] His famous reference to the "last three feet" confirms his thinking that personal interaction and frank dialogue are more valuable to a nation's long-term interests than any marketing campaign to improve its overall image in the world. That's why I think Mr. Murrow would never have approved of the ill-fated "Shared Values" advertising campaign that was initiated by the State Department after 9/11. In principle, an advertising campaign developed by Charlotte Beers and created by McCann-Erikson Worldgroup (a unit of Interpublic Group) was not a bad decision. Something had to be done after 9/11 to recalibrate America's reputation in the Middle East and Muslim countries, but an advertising campaign with a measly budget of $15 million was destined to fail. (I might add that some critics of the government would think *any* budget for such a campaign was too much.) It's not that the ads themselves didn't paint an accurate picture. It's very likely that the five Muslim Americans were completely genuine in their attitudes toward life in the United States: Rawia Ismail, Lebanese-American Mother: "In my neighborhood, all the non-Muslims, I see that they care a lot about family values just as much as I do. I didn't quite see any prejudice anywhere in my neighborhood after September 11." Abdul Hammuda, Libyan-American Businessman: "Since 9/11, we've had an overwhelming sense of support from our customers and clients. America is a land of opportunity, of equality. We are happy to live here as Muslims and preserve our faith." The five Muslim Americans featured, a baker, a schoolteacher, a paramedic, a journalism student, and a government official, all spoke of the high degree of social tolerance in the United States—an attitude about which there can be little argument. "I have co-workers who are Jewish, who are Christian, Catholic, Hindu even," said Farooq Muhammad, clad in his New York paramedic uniform, in one spot. "I have never gotten disrespect because I am a Muslim." The United States is arguably one of the most diverse and tolerant countries in the world. But is that the marketing message that the State Department needed to convey? Not unless one believes that our country was attacked on 9/11 for its social intolerance and homogeneity.

The Shared Values campaign was set to air the ads (referred to as "documentaries" by the State Department) in several Muslim countries over a five-week period, from October 28 through mid-December 2002. This time would overlap with the Muslim holy period of Ramadan, a season of inner reflection and tuning up one's devotion to God. The target market included Indonesia—the world's largest Muslim nation— Egypt, Lebanon, and Jordan, where surveys showed substantial anti-American sentiment. The marketing meltdown began when three key targets, Egypt, Lebanon and Jordan, collectively refused to air the commercials because their government-owned television did not allow airing of paid commercial advertising from other countries. The Lebanese ambassador to the United States, Farid Abboud, said, "We shouldn't run messages on behalf of other governments." The refusal to air the ads proved that the State Department and its commercial advertising firm-for-hire had failed to do their homework. Another marketing misstep was the missed opportunity to air these commercials on the most important television medium in the Middle East, Al Jazeera TV, which would have accepted the ads at a cost of only $10,000 in prime-time one-minute spots. (In comparison, a 30-second spot on Super Bowl Sunday 2003 cost $2.1 million). The State Department decided that Al Jazeera TV was just too expensive an endeavor, but this bureaucratic cost-cutting decision was made long before the embarrassment of the main target markets' refusal to air the ads. There is also the high hurdle of advertising America to a world, whether Muslim or not, increasingly weary of American advertising campaigns in general. Advertising is considered a subset of any definition of propaganda, and many overseas markets, including Islamic markets, see themselves in competition with the overwhelming presence of American advertising. So adding more advertising, this time sponsored by Uncle Sam, could easily backfire. In their book, *Propaganda and Persuasion*, Garth Jowett and Victoria O'Donnell note that "there is little doubt that under any definition of propaganda, the practice of advertising would have to be included." They define advertising "as a series of appeals, symbols, and statements deliberately designed to influence the receiver of the message toward the point of view desired by the communicator and to act in some specific way as a result of receiving the message, whether it be to purchase, vote, hold positive or negative views, or merely to maintain a memory...advertising is not always in the best interest of the receiver."[91] To some critics in the United States who first saw the ads, the content was in no one's interest, sender or receiver. Youssef Ibrahim, a senior fellow with the Council on Foreign Relations, the most prominent United States think tank dealing withforeign affairs, remarked that, "It was like this was the 1930s and the government was running commercials showing happy blacks in America. It is the policy we have to explain. You have to grab the bull by the horn and the bull is, 'Hey, here's our policy and there are good reasons for it,' instead of saying, 'Gee, there are a lot of happy Muslim people here.'"[92] Ultimately, the Shared Values campaign illustrated an administration that fundamentally misunderstood the "target market" of the Islamic world and thought that a little sugarcoating could go a long way toward explaining a very complicated story. Spotlighting five different Muslim Americans in one to two minute segments who speak glowingly about life and religious freedom in the United States is nice and friendly but begs the question: Does the average Arab or Muslim on the planet really care or wonder about how well Muslims in America are living? They may be interested in knowing how real Americans live their lives versus the Hollywood version that overpowers their impressions. But a one to two minute ad spot cannot overcome the powerhouse of tinseltown anyway. It's more likely that such a Muslim living overseas is concerned with how United States policy impacts his own life; but at best misperceived, and at worst misguided, foreign policies cannot be overcome by superficial ad campaigns. Even the ads' accompanying Web site, Common Ground, suggests that the marketing campaign was not well thought through and masks deeper schisms between the United States and the Islamic world.[93] Troubling, too, is the timing of the ads, released on the heels of a Zogby public opinion survey in eight Muslim countries that showed anti-American sentiment on the rise. Most people, it would seem, continue to strongly dislike American policies in the world.

Videos portraying life as positive for Muslims in the United States answer a question that the world is not asking and avoid providing what the world wants to know, namely, answers to critical questions about the United States' foreign policy. The world's Islamic communities may not necessarily hate the American people per se, but many have a strong antipathy to the American government. A feel-good advertisement under the guise of a documentary that is paid for and sponsored by that institution of enmity cannot overcome the bad image that the United States has in the world as a result of its domineering foreign policy, use of military violence, cultural influence, and economic projection. While it is naive to assume that the U.S. State Department is going to produce documentaries that directly address negative global public opinion about the United States' invasion and occupation of Iraq, perceived inability to treat Israeli and Palestinian atrocities equally, and proxy United States support for despotic regimes like that of Saudi Arabia, it seems little to ask that our government begin to take its global viewing audience more seriously than these videos assume.

The world outside is much more politically sophisticated and media-savvy about United States culture than we've so far given it credit and can see through what comes across as too self-serving and propagandistic. The United States is the number-one host country in the world for international students, including Muslims from other countries. As a Muslim Fulbright graduate student from Turkey said in my class after observing clips of the ads, "Muslim people are not angry with the United States because of its policies on the Muslim people living in America. We all know that America treats its citizens very well and the United States is really one of the best places to live. The Muslim world is mainly concerned about the negative political, social, and economic effects of United States policies on them. Those political issues are never addressed by the United States government."

Further, anti-Americanism is not on the rise solely in Muslim and Arab countries. Recent surveys of our close allies in Europe and elsewhere suggest that the United States government comes across as overly aggressive, condescending, and showing little interest in how others regard the United States and its policies. Using reputation-building ads in an exclusive "target market" of the Muslim world may reinforce a perception in those countries that the United States is singling out Muslim nations as the exclusive breeding ground for terrorists, when in fact, European allies have harbored terrorists for decades. Should the United States therefore extend a Shared Values campaign to the entire planet?

The marketing campaign was coordinated at the upper levels of the United States government in the office of Charlotte Beers, under secretary of state for public diplomacy and public affairs at the State Department. Charlotte Beers has stated on the record that a "30 percent conversion rate for Muslims would represent a sales curve any corporation would envy," which is ad-speak for converting anti-American Muslims to pro-American. (She might even settle on converting former anti-American Muslims to a level of indifference.) Such language of conversion is patronizing and paints billions of diverse people who share one faith with a wide brush. It is also counterproductive to repairing America's image in the world in that it sends a one-way message that it is somehow just those Muslims outside the United States who need attitude adjusting, not anyone here.

Ultimately, the Shared Values campaign failed because it ignored what seems to be the most fundamental marketing and persuasion principle—know your target audience. Even a well-thought-out marketing plan, which this one wasn't, will fail if the target market doesn't want or need "the product."

If we really want a genuine campaign to improve the image of the United States overseas we need to begin by changing our foreign policies—the source of much antipathy. And we need to find ways for the people of the United States—not just the government and big business—to carry the heavier load of representing the diversity of United States views, values, and interests abroad. As I pointed out earlier, efforts to overcome the rise in anti-Americanism that fuel both verbal and violent attacks need to spring from the grassroots of America, an "American Street" counterpart to the "Arab Street." For the majority of Americans who are nonmilitary and nonfederal government employees, the United States needs an active constituency of citizen diplomats who work to build mutual understanding between the people of the United States and the people of other nations, not just Muslim and Arab. Call it the "other" GDP (Global Dialogue Project). It's private citizens of the United States who are more comfortable with acknowledging and discussing with some degree of humility the mistakes that the United States has made in its past. Government officials seem to have a hard time with that one. And while openness to criticism of a country's policies tends to embarrass its leaders initially, over time such a willingness can be the trump card in the deck of negotiating a peaceful (and lasting) settlement of global conflicts. The American people can better initiate direct contact with people in other countries whose support and understanding we need on the stage of world opinion. The American people are frankly, in a better position to listen more and talk less. It's those last three feet— personal contact, one citizen talking to another and actively listening to each other's concerns—that can overcome communication gaps and build a bridge of understanding. No two-minute ad is going to do it.

Along with international newspapers, a number of existing United States–based international nongovernmental organizations could move along a Global Dialogue Project, including Sister Cities International, Rotary International USA, the Fulbright Alumni Association, and the International Visitors Council, an independent affiliate that works closely with the U.S. State Department's International Visitors Program. Such a project would need to extend both binational and global partnerships, so that the mistakes of the Shared Values Campaign may never reoccur.. Every mid-size American city has a mosque with a congregation likely full of citizens concerned about the declining relationship that the United States government has with many Islamic nations. So far, these faith communities have been underutilized in the persuasion battlefront of the war on terrorism. This may be due in part to the fact that the United States has yet to suffer further large-scale attacks on our "homeland" since September 11, 2001. It's critical that the third sector—civil society (noncommercial, nongovernmental groups)—step up to the plate and become a more visible force in campaigns that seeks to both improve

United States policies and that seeks mutual understanding in order to improve relations between the United States and the rest of the world—a noble enough cause. At present, many of the organizations named remain resource-poor, but they are rich in social networks, and even a doubling of their membership or a formal campaign to promote mutual understanding is better than doing nothing at all.

The world has received its fair share of the *official* American story. It is time for the U.S. government to emphasize the concept of "public" in its public-diplomacy efforts. The Shared Values advertisements for the Muslim world were just a baby step in a long walk toward better relations between the United States and the world. Public diplomacy from inside the Washington beltway is a necessary component to prevent terrorism, but it is insufficient to overcome an incomplete picture that we have of others and they have of us. What I learned from my two-year stint at USIA in the early 1990s was that there is no substitute for human storytelling over packaged information. The hard-sell approach that the U.S. Information Agency adopted at the end of the Cold War made it vulnerable to elimination as a mini–Commerce Department. Ultimately the USIA was officially abolished in 1999 and public-diplomacy placed on the back burner. The people of the United States need to tell their own stories. And the more interesting story is not just America's to tell. It must include Murrow's last three feet—sitting across the table from those who wish to tell us, the people of the United States, their stories of who they are, what they are all about, and how they live in different parts of the world. One small but proven way to better fulfill Murrow's vision would be to expand the fifty-seven-year-old Fulbright program, which for international students and scholars means a free ticket to receiving a master's or doctoral degree at an American university. Every year, about 2,200 students and scholars come to the United States to study through sponsorship of the United States government's flagship Fulbright program. An additional 1,125 grants are awarded annually to allow American students to study in foreign countries. What the government achieves through this program is a genuine affection for and lasting support of the United States, if not all its policies, its generosity and people. The program began in 1946 under legislation introduced by Sen. J. William Fulbright of Arkansas, a former Rhodes scholar who saw the value in person-to-person education for global understanding. The official goal of the Fulbright program has never altered throughout the Cold War and now the War on Terror: to "increase mutual understanding between the people of the United States and the people of other countries." A tenfold increase in the Fulbright program would cost less than one new warship, but Fulbright alumni like myself don't have the clout of a Boeing or McDonnell Douglas. It's my belief that only through expanding such personal contact can we hope to build lasting mutual understanding, a crucial component in a bigger strategy shift that may build the better image that official Washington desperately seeks.

The Myth of the Lone Dissenter

☐ ☐ ☐

JUST THREE DAYS AFTER the terrorist attacks on New York and Washington, D.C., the U.S. Congress voted unanimously in favor of issuing President Bush carte blanche support in the war on terrorism. The resolution that was put before Congress on September 14, 2001, was very simple and straightforward, but it had very far-reaching applications: "The President is authorized to use all necessary and appropriate force against those nations, organizations, or persons he determined planned, authorized, or aided the terrorist attacks that occurred on September 11, 2001 or harbored such organizations or persons." It did not seem troubling at the time that such a resolution was relinquishing the Constitutional role of the legislature to maintain a check and balance on the executive use of force.

Understandably, the nation at the time was in no mood for debate and dissension. The country was in a collective state of shock, with some cries for immediate vengeance on any Arab or Muslim Headlines were of a size unseen since World War II. Thousands of innocent men and women had been killed while going about their business. The attacks were brought to us live as we were watching morning television. It was a surprise attack on a nation's sense of security, its economy, and its institutions of government and finance.

The nation was still reeling in emotion—its own shock

and awe—and no one in the legislative branch dared to question the executive branch's use of force in going after not only those responsible for 9/11 but also those nations that might support future attacks. Members of Congress had attended a memorial service at the National Cathedral in Washington, D.C., on September 14, 2001, to coincide with a National Day of Mourning. Everyone was in utter grief, including a relatively obscure female member of Congress from Oakland, California, whose chief of staff had just lost his cousin, Wanda Green, on Flight 93—the hijacked airliner that had crashed near Pittsburgh, Pennsylvania.

In Washington, cries of tears throughout the week were turning into cries of anger. Bomb them (whoever they are) back to the Stone Age. Eliminate those who attacked us. The country was speaking in one voice—we must act and strike back. Only one woman dared to question this unanimity, the Congressional woman who attended that Friday memorial service along with her chief of staff and wondered if she could possibly raise an objection to the president who mourned with her that day in the Cathedral. She couldn't forget the words of the Bishop: "We must not become the evil we deplore." It was that statement that formed her decision.

The vote to use force in retaliation against the 9/11 attacks was scheduled for Saturday, September 15, 2001, but the Republican majority in Congress rescheduled it for the evening of the memorial service. It was a move that capitalized on the emotional climate of that day in American history. One woman looked down that evening at two voting buttons, one red and one green. She pressed red. The daughter of a Korean War veteran and self-described army brat, Democratic Congresswoman Rep. Barbara Lee, would quickly come to realize that she had cast the vote heard round the world. Her Congressional Web site was soon receiving e-mail invectives labeling her a commie and a traitor and plain-clothes Capitol police hovered near her Washington office in response to death threats from fellow Americans. Anti-war activists rallied around her as a hero to the American tradition of dissent in times of war, whose symbolic act was vitally important in a democracy, where one may question the president and his unbridled use of force. Lee's defiance of the fashion of the day, a nation united but unquestioning, made Republicans vow to take her out in the next election, spurred on by on-air diatribes against her by Rush Limbaugh (who, in fairness, months later did approve her stance in favor of the rights of Congress). A "Dump Barbara Lee" Web site sprang up, which for a time ran a photograph of a grinning Barbara Lee superimposed over the image of the burning Twin Towers. She was quickly dubbed the lone dissenter and marginalized by most as completely un-American in her questioning of the President in time of crisis. I saw her as an American super-woman from the very beginning.

On January 14, 2002, one day before the anniversary of the birthday of Reverend Martin Luther King, Jr., I had the opportunity to meet Barbara Lee when she was in town to deliver remarks at a Town Hall Los Angeles luncheon. Like so many other lookyloos in the audience, we were eager to see how she would be received as the "lone dissenter" in Congress. As an African-American woman from Oakland, California, the birthplace of the Black Panther movement, I could only imagine what some critics were undoubtedly still thinking of Barbara Lee as an African-American woman from Oakland, California, the birthplace of the Black Panther movement—, namely, who does this "uppity black woman" think she is, to dare question President Bush?

I expected a more aggressive, even a strident critic of the President, but Barbara Lee was very soft-spoken and polite in her delivery. She opened her remarks in an almost prayerful manner: "Since that terrible day, we are slowly recovering from our profound sense of shock...We are forever changed by that tragedy, but we take more from it than searing memories. We must really emerge with an even stronger faith in democracy, our Constitution, and our fellow human beings. We must come out of this conflict more dedicated to peace, more aware of the world around us and more secure." To Barbara Lee, the U.S. Congress represented the deliberative body of the United States government, the rational mind of the body politic. It and the Constitution must act as a brake on excessive tyranny. If it were to hold on to that function, it must stay above any emotion of the moment and make decisions that can stand the test of time. Lee thought that the Bush administration had transferred power from the hands of the legislators to the executive branch in part through a deft manipulation of the emotional climate of a nation in mourning and in search of swift punishment.

What fascinated me even more about Barbara Lee's courageous vote was the manner in which the major news media had "framed" her as a voice in the wilderness regarding the executive use of force. In truth, she *was* the only member of Congress to vote against giving up legislative control of the use of force to the executive branch. However, she was no lone dissenter in the opposition to the war approach on terrorism. At the time of her vote, she was supported all over the world by masses of people who prefer peaceful options to using war as a means of punishment. And certainly her vote was in keeping with a long history in the United States of peace and social-justice movements. One might have thought history had blown away in the wind, given most of the press coverage of Barbara Lee's vote. She was treated like a pariah or an alien from outer space. The treatment she received was in keeping with some of most fundamental propaganda techniques of the modern era.

Before the start of World War II, the Institute for Propaganda Analysis (IPA) was established in the United States by Edward Filene of Filene's Basement, who, along with other prominent businesspeople and academics of the day, was frustrated with media manipulations. IPA was founded in October 1937 "to conduct objective, nonpartisan studies in the field of propaganda and public opinion...it seeks to help the intelligent citizen to detect and to analyze propaganda, by revealing the agencies, techniques, and devices used by the propagandist."[94] IPA disseminated its research through monthly bulletins, special reports, adult-education programs, and curricula for high schools and colleges. IPA disbanded after the United States entered World War II but left behind many publications that continue to inform what we know now about how propaganda influences our thoughts and actions. The organization is most famous for identifying the seven key propaganda devices most commonly practiced: (1) Name Calling: associating an idea with a bad label; (2) Card Stacking: literally "to stack the cards" for or against an idea by selective use of facts or logic; (3) Bandwagon: to give the impression that the idea is supported by everyone; (4) Testimonial: associating a person of some respected authority (doctor) or visibility (celebrity) with the idea; (5) Plain Folks: associating an idea's merit with its being "of the people"; (6) Transfer: carrying the prestige or disapproval of something over to something else such as displaying the American flag as an emotional transfer device to represent one's patriotism; (7) Glittering Generality: associating something with a virtue word; opposite of name-calling (freedom, democracy); often used to make us accept a concept without thoroughly examining its application.

For purposes of illustration, I've chosen extracts from two articles about Barbara Lee, one by the Voice of America bureau chief who covered her appearance in Los Angeles in January 2002, and another, by Herbert Romerstein, that appeared in the *Washington Times* on September 18, 2001, under the heading, "Who is Barbara Lee?"[95] Both use a potpourri of propaganda devices that show language tricks to shortcut thought and reason from more emotionally laden persuasive techniques.

Mr. Romerstein starts out with a plain-folks and bandwagon approach: "Most Americans have never heard of Rep. Barbara Lee, California Democrat—the only member of the House of Representatives to vote against supporting President Bush's plan to use military force in response to the terrorist attack." She is immediately marginalized as someone out of step with the rest of us good plain-folk Americans who support the President. Romerstein immediately compares Lee to "the eccentric Jeanette Rankin, the congresswoman who voted against both World Wars I and II." What makes Jeannette Rankin eccentric we'll never know, but Rankin is used as a name-calling device to get the reader to reject the legitimacy of Lee's vote without examining the rationale for it. To Romerstein, Lee is even worse than Rankin. Whereas "the pacifist Rankin hated war, but did not love either the Kaiser or Adolf Hitler...Ms. Lee is a long-practicing supporter of America's enemies—from Fidel Castro on down." Romerstein's choice of words makes Lee sound like a religious convert ("long-practicing") to unnamed individuals or groups; he employs a transfer technique to carry the disapproval of Castro over to Lee, thereby sullying her reputation. Think of transfer as a guilt-by-association method of character bashing. How does Lee specifically support Castro? Who are those American enemies on whom she practices her support? She admires and often quotes Martin Luther King, Jr., in her speeches, but Romerstein makes no mention of that. Romerstein says only that "In Congress, Ms. Lee spoke up in support of Fidel Castro." His commentary makes no effort to honestly portray the "real" Barbara Lee.

"Ms. Lee," he writes, "told *The Progressive* magazine that her life was influenced by the late Carlton Goodlet. That explains a lot. Goodlet was a dedicated Stalinist and served in the leadership of the international Soviet front, the World Peace Council.... In 1981, Ms. Lee wrote to the World Peace Council asking that the Soviet front pay for air tickets for California Rep. Ron Dellums and two staffers to attend one of their conferences." This section uses the card-stacking device—selectively using facts to present the worst-case scenario for a program, person, or product. President Nixon traveled to China and the Soviet Union, and President Ronald Reagan held regular summit meetings with the known Communist, Mikhail Gorbachev. But Lee's use of airline tickets to a "Soviet front" conference is enough information, it seems, to reinforce her un-American proclivities. Perhaps she, like many in the 1980s, had a great concern that the United States and the Soviet Union would engage in nuclear war and supported peaceful coexistence over confrontation. We don't get any useful background information other than the most simple name-calling words that are peppered throughout Romerstein's article, words like "leftwing," "leftist," "Stalinist," "Trotskyite" "communist-ruled" (in reference to Grenada) and "pacifist," which are used as shortcut character references to the fundamental question at hand, "Who is Barbara Lee?"

He sums up her entire character in the following: "While she stands out as an extremist in Congress, Ms. Lee fits in well with the Oakland–San Francisco leftist fever swamps that have produced so many bizarre political ideas. The public radio and Pacifica radio station in the area has carried one commentator after another blaming the United States for causing the terrorist act. Sometimes it's our support for Israel, but often enough it's just being America that is used to justify the attack on our country." He ends by saying that "while most of the left-wing Democrats spent the week praising President Bush and trying to sound as moderate as possible, Barbara Lee continued to sail under her true colors." Romerstein uses his references to President Bush as a glittering generality device, which associates something, in this case the President, with a virtue word or concept, to make us accept and approve the thing without question. The virtuous President Bush is compared to his opposite, an obviously unrighteous person like Lee, who is clearly out of step with the mainstream patriotic Americans who aren't part of the "blame America first" camp.

Finally, Romerstein's credentials are used at the end of the editorial as a testimonial device that he is an expert and authority figure on the American character, particularly the ability to distinguish patriots from enemies of the United States government: "Herbert Romerstein served on the professional staff of the House Intelligence Committee and as the head of the Office of Counter Soviet Disinformation at the U.S. Information Agency. His latest book, *The Venona Secrets: Exposing Soviet Espionage and America's Traitors*, was recently published by Regnery."

The Voice of America piece by Mike O'Sullivan, who covered Lee's Town Hall presentation, uses the same bandwagon device in the articles' headline, "Lone Dissenter on Anti-Terrorism Resolution Draws Support," which immediately implies that Rep. Lee still hasn't "gotten with the program" or the bandwagon thinking on the war. The name-calling reference to the "lone dissenter" indicates that some four months after 9/11 Barbara Lee still operated outside the mainstream and cannot therefore be thoroughly trusted as an authority figure. "The lone dissenter...continues to defend her position." Not only is she alone on the issue but she's obstinate too! Her "sympathetic audience in Los Angeles" carries a negative transfer device. Los Angeles is associated with liberal ideas, Hollywood values (amoral, immoral), and a life outside the mainstream. Further, the picture implied is of the rough-and-tumble urban environment, not one of the plain folks, who have the values of the countryside. This is a woman giving a speech on the Left Coast who's drawing support from the usual suspects who reside there. Read on.

The entire Voice of America VOA piece about Barbara Lee uses a tone of disbelief and surprise. A card-stacking device is used with the following statement: "It is said nothing succeeds like success, and the overthrow of the Taliban and routing of the Al Qaeda network in Afghanistan is proof for most Americans that the decision to use force there was a wise one." It is not clear at all by what measure that success is being determined. Is success measured by a lack of casualties on the American side of the equation? Osama Bin Laden and Mullah Muhammad Omar are all still at large, and Taliban insurgents are regrouping in Afghanistan and continue attacking. A careful examination of the evidence in Afghanistan would draw different conclusions. These details are omitted so that the reader will draw the rightful conclusion, namely that a full "House" of Barbara Lees might have impaired the implied success of the military campaign in Afghanistan. In fact, perhaps her go-slow approach might have made the campaign even more successful by locating those directly responsible through working with local intelligence instead of dropping bombs that killed Afghan citizens.

The article's theme includes the bandwagon effect that everybody, at least all the reasonable folks, are supporting the war effort: "September 14, just three days after the terror attacks in New York and Washington she alone voted 'no'"—which implies a lack of proper emotional support, perhaps even patriotism, for the country's effort to punish those responsible for these vicious attacks. O'Sullivan leaves out Rep. Lee's compelling argument in her Town Hall speech for taking a measured response in light of so much emotion and shock just three days after the attacks. "Like everyone, I was angry. That did not mean that I believed that the U.S. Congress, with little evidence, little information, and almost no debate, should give the executive branch broad authority to potentially wage war against more than 60 nations. Our Constitution is based on fundamental principles. The separation of powers is absolutely central to our system of government. That system depends on each branch of government upholding its responsibilities and authority. Congress was not voting to declare war; it was voting to give almost unlimited authority to the President to pursue the perpetrators of September 11th and any of their supporters anywhere. I could not support such a broad, open-ended grant of war-making power."

Finally, testimonials are used in strategic ways. To perhaps show some media balance in how she was portrayed by the press, Voice of America VOA reporter O'Sullivan includes the following statement: "One conservative commentator has called the congresswoman an anti-American communist and a traitor." This person went unnamed, although that person was Rush Limbaugh who until his recent scandal was both respected and highly admired in conservative circles and vilified in others. Those who know about Rush Limbaugh are not neutral in their opinions of him. Perhaps Limbaugh's name calling was considered so vociferous that the VOA writer chose to keep him anonymous. While Limbaugh was-n't identified by name in the article, another person received much attention in the piece: "The noted feminist Gloria Steinem is there and she supports the Congresswoman." Steinem is given an inordinate amount of attention in the article, and her picture is included. The use of Steinem's name and accompanying photo carries two propaganda devices—transfer and testimonial. Given the alleged public disapproval of Lee's vote, a negative association is implied to show that Steinem is a supporter of Rep. Lee. The hidden message is that Lee is out of step with the mainstream and may also be a mil-itant or radical feminist, since there are no designated "mod-erate" feminists in the media.

The art and science of propaganda analysis is to examine the evidence. This process requires taking a long look at words and the way they are combined to build support for or against an idea or program. Propaganda techniques aim to evoke non-rational emotional impulses so that we will issue immediate judgment calls on the guilt or innocence of the program, idea, or person. In a propaganda environment, the best defense is a good defense. Guard against mental shortcuts and ask your-self important questions: What is the speaker or writer really implying? Are there any hidden motives or appeals to the emotions? How are words being used to imply something not overtly stated? Propaganda has its limits when countered by critical thinking.

In reality, Barbara Lee's single vote was a symbol for ongo-ing peace and social-justice movements in the United States that so far have been characterized by the master narrative of the Bush administration as out of step and therefore out of view of the "one nation, one mind" sentimentality. Why was Rep. Lee such a threat if she was the lone dissenter? She dared to call for using peace to fight terrorism, and this message did not fit within the narrow war framework that the Bush admin-istration was putting in place within hours of the 9/11 attacks. In this case, if the message doesn't fit, you must convict!

As Lee told our Town Hall gathering, "Nowhere in this resolution were there reporting requirements that Congress had included in the Gulf War Resolution that there might be some oversight of the Executive branch by Congress. Unlike any past declaration of war or use of force resolution, there was really no country or region named. The scope was global, the time-frame infinite. It was really overly broad and vague." Her rationale for voting against H.J. Res. 64 seems measured, rational, and constitutionally grounded. The message was clear enough and could have called on the collective con-sciousness of America to suspend judgment until thoroughly exhausting all options of responding. Because the Executive branch had decided almost immediately after the attacks to employ a war option,[96] the messenger had to be vilified in order to deflect attention from the message.

What a contrast the Voice of America and *Washington Times* articles are to the exchange Barbara Lee had with Bill Hogan of the progressive *Mother Jones* magazine just ten days after September 11, 2001, when the criticism of Lee's vote had reached a crescendo:

> MOTHER JONES: Last Friday night, on the House floor, you cited Wayne Morse, one of two senators who voted against the 1964 Gulf of Tonkin resolu-tion, which gave President Lyndon Johnson the power to wage war in Vietnam. You quoted Morse as saying, "I believe that history will record that we have made a grave mistake in subverting and cir-cumventing the Constitution of the United States." Then you added: "Senator Morse was correct, and I

fear we make the same mistake today." But don't you think that there's a loss of institutional memory on Capitol Hill, that there are Members of Congress who would say, "Wayne who?"

REP. LEE: Oh, yes. So much today is poll-driven. You know, we need people to become empowered at this moment, now that our civil liberties are being eroded. We need people to become more involved in the political process. I believe that firmly. I wish the press were paying more attention to the erosion of the Constitution and the slippery slope that we're getting into, by giving up the right of the Congress to talk about when and how and where we go to war. I don't think that's been covered enough, and it should be. That's an important right to preserve in a state of national crisis such as this.

Wayne Morse is another hero of Barbara Lee's, and he, along with Martin Luther King, Jr., went unmentioned in the two articles I analyzed. Morse, who represented Oregon, noted at the time of his dissenting vote, "I don't know why we think, just because we're mighty, we have the right to try to substitute might for right." Also unmentioned was the fact that Lee has a master's degree in social welfare from UC-Berkeley, one of the nation's preeminent institutions of higher learning. The cries of "commie traitor" that surrounded Barbara Lee in the aftermath of 9/11 should prompt us to ask how often we make judgments solely on the basis of what we read or what someone tells us is true. One personal story Lee shared with the London *Independent* casts more light into the soul of this anything-but-lone dissenter: "I remember very clearly going to restaurants with my family, and the waitress or waiter telling us, 'We don't serve...' and then they'd use the N-word, and we'd have to leave. I remember wanting to go to public theaters with my friends who were Latino and white, and I couldn't go because blacks weren't allowed. My Mother told me this story as a child. When she was in labor and about to deliver me, they refused to let her in the hospital because she was black. Really, they left her to die. Finally my grandmother got her admitted; she was supposed to have a C-section but by then it was too late. So they had to take me out using a forceps, and I had a scar above my eyes for many years. I literally came into the world fighting to survive."[97]

If anything, Barbara Lee is the ultimate survivor, for her vote against giving the administration a blank check on the use of force is being vindicated in the postwar chaos in Iraq. Why didn't more Barbara Lee types step forward in the fall of 2001 to have a full congressional debate and examination of the "imminent threat" explanation by the White House before nonchalantly supporting the President's use of force in Iraq? The American people were showing their shift of support toward Barbara Lee's gallant questioning of the facts at hand. In one *Washington Post*–ABC News poll in mid-August 2002, three-quarters of the American people surveyed thought Bush should seek the approval of Congress before going to war with Iraq.[98] He got his approval for the war in Iraq by that unanimous vote of Congress on September 14, 2001, which was cosmetically enhanced by a congressional vote in October 2002. Barbara Lee, true to her spirit on September 14, 2001, voted against the war with Iraq, and she has become a hero to the progressive side of the electorate that continues to question its executive leadership. No lone dissenter, she is supported by a growing movement of ordinary citizens and peace and social-justice activists who may very well affect the outcome of the presidential election in 2004.

Uncle Sam and the "Arab Street"

□ □ □

ONE WEEK INTO THE WAR with Iraq, CNN State Department correspondent Andrea Koppel addressed the Bush administration's public-diplomacy efforts in the Middle East. "The Bush administration finds itself in a pitched battle for hearts and minds, not only in Iraq, but on an increasingly angry Arab street."[99] Since 9/11, the "Arab street" had become a common catchall phrase in the media for Arab citizens whose opinion of the United States is crucial in retaining influence in the region. It also referred to those Al Jazeera–supplied pictures of people literally taking to the streets chanting and screaming in protest of United States policies. The term "Arab street" seemed to position a region of the world as particularly prone to mob rule. There was no Soviet street, Chinese street, or even Canadian street, so why the Arab street? I came to believe that part of the United States' problem with the Arab region was that the language we used in talking about it was overly paternalistic and stereotypical— that is, racist. Millions of Americans would hear or read about the Arab street in the media and assume that it meant a place where terrorism flourished, danger lurked around every corner, and religious and political fanaticism were the norm. The way it is often presented, the Arab street could not possibly produce people with a healthy attitude toward the United States. It underscores a bigoted view in the West that Arabs are incapable of self-government because they lack sufficient logic to organize society out of so much chaos. And that bigoted view can only feed, rather than prevent, bigoted acts, especially in the aftermath of 9/11. In 2000, the FBI received reports of 28 hate crimes against Muslims and Arabs in the United States. In 2001, that number increased to 481.[100]

With an Arab street foremost on its mind, how could the U.S. State Department or the White House employ effective foreign policy or public diplomacy in the region? And why not use a more sophisticated measure, like Arab public opinion or Arab citizen response, which might shift thinking away from paternalism to possibility? Since I'm not a Middle East regional expert and could only theorize my own answers to these questions, I sought out two diverse perspectives on the so-called Arab street, one American, and one Syrian, both providing a range of perceptions on how Uncle Sam might engage the region.

Richard Alan Nelson is a professor in the Manship School of Mass Communications, Louisiana State University, and the author of *A Chronology and Glossary of Propaganda in the United States* (Greenwood, 1996). Professor Nelson is a leading propaganda scholar in the United States. He and I share a common understanding of propaganda, namely, that most Americans are ambivalent about it. On the one hand, the American public knows that the United States is a world leader in the arena of mass persuasion regarding our global political, economic, and cultural dominance. On the other hand, propaganda has come to connote deception, manipulation, and an association with totalitarian regimes, like those of Hitler and Stalin. The American people would rather not accept the idea that Uncle Sam might resort to the same communication tactics as the most despicable figures in the twentieth century. For the most part, the American public accepts the concept that the darker side of information control is carried out only during wartime and directed only at enemies. It's harder to accept the fact that to a free and open society like the United States, propaganda is as American as apple pie. The inalienable right to communicate, whether to persuade or not, is enshrined in the First Amendment to the Constitution. The propaganda industries in the United States run the gamut from the technologies and business models of mass media that have influenced global culture, through political campaign commercials and opposition research, to the professional practitioners of mass influence in marketing and advertising that affect the behavior of individual consumers in a mass society. Whereas propaganda may have come of age in the twentieth century, its refinement, its efforts to use information to maintain and build social cohesion and control defines the twenty-first century.

This control is often hidden from view because ever since 1948, the United States government has prohibited the domestic dissemination of propaganda meant for foreign populations. Known as the the Smith-Mundt Act of 1948, this "propaganda for them, not us" approach to United States information-war programs was an outgrowth of two previous administrations, Wilson's Committee on Public Information and Truman's Campaign of Truth. The original intent of the law was to protect the American public from propaganda techniques that were designed to influence ambivalent publics overseas or campaigns targeting enemies of the United States. Since 9/11, it's become more transparent to some that, Smith-Mundt aside, what is effective on "them" is just as effective on "us." Despite the February 2002 aborted Office of Strategic Influence in the Department of Defense, more recently the White House has initiated its new P.R. offensive by Bush, Cheney, Rice, and Rumsfeld to target friendlier and more receptive American media and communities about how much better things are going in Iraq than was earlier thought.

In April 2002, I interviewed Professor Nelson at the fourteenth annual conference of the International Academy of Business Disciplines, where we spoke at a session titled "Communicating a Controversial Message: Propaganda and Public Affairs." Nelson's presentation was a post–September 11 analysis of United States government efforts to influence the "Arab street." The following is an excerpt of his remarks in answer to my question.

Explain what you mean by United States government efforts to influence the "Arab street"?

The Arab street[101] is a term that refers to the masses in Arab society who are forced to take to the streets to express themselves. It's the only way they get counted in public opinion and have a chance to influence news. The Intifada and human bombers are seen as a frustrated and violent extension of these street protests. The problem that the United States government has is that it has never really seriously cared about the street and the people who live there. It's never seriously invested time to make relations, mostly for neglectful reasons. When you look at the demographics of a majority of Arabs, it would be a teenager who only speaks one language [Arabic] and has a relatively low level of education.[102] That's a demographic reality within the Arab society. It is still very diverse within the Arab world, with different interpretations of the Koran, Shiite and Sunni Muslims, etcetera. More than that, you have states like Qatar, Dubai, the United Arab Emirates that are prosperous and are investing their money in infrastructure, education, and women's education. Then you have other countries like Libya, where under Colonel

Qaddafi the quality of life has actually improved to the highest ever experienced by the population there, but he never gets any credit for that.

Why the neglect?

From where does the United States Government get its information of the Arab and Muslim world? Mostly from the diplomatic corps and the intelligence/law-enforcement communities, all of which have serious structural weaknesses. One key problem is that they don't often speak the language. It's amazing how very few United States representatives know Arabic. Domestically, we haven't used our melting-pot demographics; we have a huge and growing Muslim and Arab population within the United States, and the United States government hasn't been recruiting actively out of that until very recently. The same problems are reflected in our State Department. It's still very Euro-centric with very CFR-type (Council on Foreign Relations) people.

In addition, the United States government is getting information about the Arab and Muslim world from the educated classes who speak English and from English-language media. That leaves out the large majority of the people. In a country like Egypt, the information structure is like a T, with the top of the T representing a wealthy and educated class and the stem of the T representing a large majority of people who have nothing or close to nothing in resources. The top tier has some good people but it's difficult for them to make the kind of changes through traditional means of communication when you don't have a culture of democracy that supports reform.

Despite some humanitarian funding, most of the monies spent in the region are targeted for military purposes. Ironically, the United States is the world's largest arms exporter, and this cannot help to promote demilitarization. Unfortunately, the evidence is clear that the United States government has not actively supported democracy and human rights in the Arab world because policymakers have felt that is counter to United States interests in the region.

How can the United States best influence the Arab Street in a post-9/11 environment?
I argue that you have to first clearly define what the United States' interests are. There is a growing split between what the government policymakers are proclaiming is their national interest and what really is the national interest of the average working and educated person in America.

As part of this, I really believe we need "New Think" (to use an Orwellian term) to reevaluate the whole nature of our relationship to the Middle East, what our relationship is with Israel, and what role our arms shipments play as a primary exporter to these potentially volatile countries. Every dollar spent on questionable military purposes, for example, is one that is not available for investment elsewhere (fixing educational problems at home, for example.) Sending weapons to the region is now not particularly constructive to peace.

The United States, if it wants to influence the future, also has to move beyond a marketing model to focusing on real relationship building. It requires that we spend more money on communicating with young people in the region and listening rather than talking and dictating, which seems to be our communication style as a government. Unless the policymakers in Washington and our government representatives overseas, including the CIA, look toward addressing the legitimate aspirations of people, the United States will have problems.

Are we taking advantage of the public relations expertise within our country and overseas by people who care about building relationships?

No, not at all. We have a large community of educated Arabs in the United States who care about America, but we're not using them as effectively as we could. That is also true when looking at the recommendations made by professional public-relations practitioners. Most of these suggestions have been ignored or only given lip service. Fortunately, the United States has a foundation of support in the region that continues to exist despite all that has happened. Those who travel there sometimes are surprised at how many people overseas (including the Middle East) like individual Americans and believe in the basic principles of democracy, tolerance, and human rights. But unless we stick to our principles and remain consistent in communicating them, we are going to set up a situation where the United States is seen as a bad guy by large numbers of people. This scenario is not good for America. However, unless *we* Americans and our government officials change the way we act, the United States is going to experience further grief and fail to achieve other important foreign policy goals.

Six months out, how would you grade the government's information efforts to exert influence?

Right now, I'd give it a "D" grade. For one reason, policymakers were initially thrown into a "hurry up and wait" approach after 9/11. They didn't have the infrastructure in place, so you could see the confusion domestically and overseas. We don't yet know what role and powers the Office of Homeland Security is going to have. The United States is still spending too much time sending an inconsistent message. We see the fumbling over one another among the CIA, DEA, FBI, and other agencies. Yet I do think that officials are trying to get a handle on this now. We're still spending too much time sending an inconsistent message. We've had some successes. Some of the things we still don't know about may become useful for the United States' foreign policy. I'm not so certain when you look at United States efforts to mediate between Israel and Palestine and how that has been influenced by other communication efforts in the war on terrorism. It seems to me that the goals of the Bush administration for stability there haven't yet been met. There's a growing anger about this.

What is the United States government relationship to information control?
The administration believes in information control. Most governments orient themselves that way, particularly during wartime. They don't like leaks. The rise and fall of the Office of Strategic Influence (OSI) is an example. Press pools in Afghanistan were very tightly controlled. This lessens our ability as citizens to determine what we as citizens know, whether or not our government is doing something right or not and whether as a society we are on the right path. It's human nature to want to cover up our mistakes.

After my interview with Richard Nelson, I spoke with Hazem Ibrahim, a Fulbright scholar from Syria who was attending the same conference.[103] Hazem came to the United States in July 2000 to complete his master's degree in intercultural communication at California State University, Sacramento. He came to the United States to study communication and to answer the question, "Why do they hate us?" He wanted to find out how citizens of the world can better understand each other.

How do you define the Arab street?
I think it refers to a young population. In some Arab countries, 55–60 percent of the population is under the age of eighteen. It is a very young society, which is posing a struggle for governments in terms of how you deal with political corruption and political backwardness and instability and how you provide jobs and employment. Religion for some becomes a mental and spiritual escape route. The slogan, "Islam is the solution," is one of the most famous slogans in Muslim society because Islam is seen as a way of life in every capacity. It provides everything you need, from leadership to how you keep yourself clean. Islam is viewed as a complete way of life by some. People differ in interpretations of Islam, but militant Islamists tend to claim to have solutions for all our ills, like the Taliban in Afghanistan.

What fuels the anti-Americanism we see in the street?
In propaganda methodology, governments tend to like to pull out their foreign-enemy card when necessary. It's always easier to blame internal problems on external factors. The shadowy enemy, this illusive enemy, in this case the United States, is what some Arab governments seem to be fighting. The people pour into the streets to protest American foreign policy and its backing of Israel, but at the same time the same people may be having domestic problems sending their children to school or gaining access to clean water. People in the Arab world are in a much easier position to protest the shadowy foreign enemy when they don't have the same political rights to protest their own governments.

How do you view the United States media coverage of the Arab street?
I believe that the United States media is free (not state-con-

trolled); however, it seems a small percentage of the world is actually being covered. Media power centers seem satisfied with their coverage as long as their dominant positions remain intact. Many people do not seek alternative sources of information or don't know how to, and so it seems like the media are free in terms of nongovernment control, but the United States news is not comprehensive. As long as the major media interests are being served, they don't care about imperfections.

How do you explain the paradox of middle-class terror as illustrated by the backgrounds of the September 11 hijackers? It's easy to explain. They become frustrated in a political system in which they cannot openly express themselves. They have no political avenue. They cannot even publish an opinion in a newspaper. The Arab media are tightly controlled, with a few exceptions. Look at the websites of Human Rights Watch or Journalists Without Borders, and you'll see the numbers of Arab journalists who are being censored. The environment in which those people grow up is one in which there is no true and open political representation. Many Arab governments are largely self-interested and more or less interested in sustaining their own regimes, clout, and connections. It's about themselves. These governments use slogans that may be Islamic, pan-Arab, or nationalist, but the people who grow up with potential and education have no wide avenues for expressing themselves. There's a joke in the Arab world that can illustrate this: You say that America is a free country. You can criticize Clinton or Bush. We say that we're a free country too. We can criticize Clinton or Bush.

When you think of the September 11 hijackers and their level of education, you'd think they would be interested in giving back, like what the Fulbright program proclaims, the power of transformation through education.

Let's look at someone like Mohamed Atta, who was on a German equivalent of the Fulbright program. He studied architecture in Germany and developed a close relationship with a German professor. He was a very smart guy. It's reasonable to believe that those guys thought that they were "giving back" to their Arab societies because they viewed the United States as having gone beyond any reason in blind support over Israel to the detriment of the Arab and Muslim people. It's well documented in the Arab press that Israel and the United States jointly abstain in many United Nations General Assembly resolutions. In the Arab street, this is well known. In the United States media, you won't see this mentioned, outside of alternative sources like Noam Chomsky or Edward Said.

After talking with Hazem Ibrahim and Professor Richard Nelson, it was clear that there are not just miles and oceans between our physical proximity but also a widening gulf in our understanding of each other. Outside of what governments can do to influence their image in the world, the responsibility will remain within our global educational infrastructure.

The American struggle with the Arab region is, if not a clash of civilizations, a clash of perceptions about how societies should be organized. At the "street level" of hostile Arab public opinion and in the fundamentalist Islamic youth schools, madrassas, the United States is seen as the driving force of economic neocolonialism and Western cultural imperialism, which seeks to dominate and replace local values and traditions. This is an Arabic form of anti-American propaganda that needs challenging, but the present path of the United States toward the Arab region doesn't recognize that it is what the United States *does* in the region that really matters and how these actions are perceived, not whether or not it labels its invasion and occupation of Iraq as "liberation" or

"Operation Iraqi Freedom.") Like it or not, there will always be some who refuse to believe that the United States is, as President Bush sees our nation, "a force for good in the world." Where we may be missing the greatest opportunity for mutual understanding is in regard to the vast majority of Arab citizens, who occupy a realistic middle ground in their view of the United States and whose sons and daughters would be willing to willingly come to the U.S. on a Fulbright scholarship or otherwise engage our own youth in dialogue and debate. Support or opposition to the United States on the part of Arab youth depends both on the United States' policy and practices in the Middle East and on the perceptual framework in which these events take place. If United States foreign policy continues to be violent, militaristic, and to be oblivious to the needs of the people whose choices are desperate, it will be hard to alter the image of the United States as a Great Satan; likewise, if the United States continues to view the Arab world through the lens of "the street," then the mutual strategy for truth and credibility will continue to wane.

The Citizen, the University, and the Publisher

This is what separated us from you; we made demands.
You were satisfied to serve the power of the nation and we
dreamed of giving ours her truth.
    –ALBERT CAMUS, FROM "LETTERS TO A GERMAN FRIEND"

□ □ □

SINCE I WAS A LITTLE GIRL, I've always put teachers on a pedestal. I'll never forget my fifth-grade African-American teacher at George Washington Carver Elementary School in downtown Richmond, Virginia, telling me that I should be a writer. It made me feel so grown up and individuated. I had a greater purpose now than just taking up room breathing in the earth's oxygen. My educational environment that spanned from Lincoln Logs and recess to college-level philosophy taught me how to think and how to interact and socialize with people whose thinking was often in marked contrast to my own upbringing. For a time, as a teenager, I was a fundamentalist Christian. During that time, my feeling toward non-Christians—including immediate members of my family—was one of pity for not having seen the "light" of my higher consciousness and faith. During my college days, I remember a friend pointing out that I carried my Christian self with an air of superiority, as if my shoulders were slightly higher than everyone else's. He stopped me in my tracks. I realized that my thinking, which was couched in terms of measuring people as faithful or unfaithful, was absolutist, was damaging to how I wanted to live my life as a human being. Such dogmatism went against my educated sense of what the university experience was all about—sharing of values, civility, respect, and tolerance for others—that went beyond any textbook or classroom. From then on, teachers and professors became my primary mentors. I sought my Ph.D. so that I could combine my two loves, teaching and writing, and after a brief two-year stint doing academic research, renewed that commitment to the university classroom after 9/11. I think this is why I was so deeply disturbed by an event that took place on a university campus on December 15, 2001. Janis Besler Heaphy, publisher and president of the *Sacramento Bee*, was invited to give a commencement address at California State University at Sacramento, one that she wasn't able to complete because of the words she elected to say. It was four months almost to the day since September 11.

Heaphy chose a commencement theme that placed the role of the university as the main forum in American society for unabashed free speech and unrestrained debate. "The terrorist attacks awakened a sense of patriotism long dormant in this country. We have been reminded of our greatness and how lucky we are to be Americans. But that blessing comes with responsibilities. It is our right, our privilege, our obligation to live and uphold America's values and ideals. And it those values that I ask you to consider today." While acknowledging the need for both retaliation and homeland security after 9/11, she asked, "to what degree are we willing to compromise our civil liberties in the name of security?" Heaphy listed the USA PATRIOT Act's expansion of the government's surveillance powers and the thousands of young

Middle Eastern men in United States detention facilities who were being stripped of their due process rights. "For the most part, they go unnamed and uncharged." She placed into context several incidents of press censorship following 9/11, as when the national security adviser, Condoleezza Rice, citing security concerns, persuaded the five major television news organizations to censor portions of the videos produced by Osama Bin Laden. "Where do we draw the line? And how do news organizations maintain their credibility if the public knows government has the ability to censor news reports? If Bin Laden's words are suppressed, should we then censor the words of anyone who might oppose the Administration or disagrees with a United States policy?... Scrutiny by the press of this war on terrorism and publication of dissenting viewpoints are not signs of disloyalty. Rather, they are expressions of confidence in democracy and in the fulfillment of the First Amendment's charge to hold government accountable." While "some of our political leaders may believe that less is more when it comes to information regarding the war on terrorism...that, ladies and gentlemen, is a dangerous mindset. When information grows scant, rumor and innuendo swell to fill the void. When the press grows timid, half-truths and rhetoric pass as facts."

By that point in her speech the audience was booing her loudly, and appearing visibly shaken, she turned back to her seat. What Heaphy illustrated in her remarks, before she was booed off the stage, was a determined willingness to ask the questions that serve the citizenry, however difficult it is to ask those questions or however much they may express disagreement with our government. We may never know the motives of those who shouted and stomped. Perhaps there was a mix of those who were put off by her questioning the erosion of civil liberties in a time of war, while others may have thought that she "rained" on their day to shine. My country right or wrong meets the world is your oyster. Parents may have sought something light-hearted and uplifting, while some students may just have wanted to get the occasion over with sooner. Whatever the cause, it's the consequence of their actions that brought the university and the publisher a certain amount of fame and fallout. What it brought us as citizens was a textbook example of our democracy at work. It is Heaphy's act of dissent, her willingness to question those who derive their power from the consent of the governed, her dissent uttered in a public setting, on the campus of a university, that deserves our congratulations. Like Representative Barbara Lee, Heaphy chose the courage of her convictions to ask the difficult questions when the expected thing was to stay politely silent. And the saddest part is that the uplifting section of her speech came at its conclusion, which she was never able to deliver:

> As you, the graduates, prepare to take your place in society, I want to challenge you to be active participants in the democratic process. To exercise your rights as Americans...means staying educated about the issues. Listen to the radio. Watch television. Read newspapers, magazines, books. Be inquisitive. Remember, asking questions about government policies isn't disloyal. It's your duty. Once you've developed your opinions, have the courage to express them. Freedom of expression is one of our most cherished American values. It sets us apart. It makes us great...but it can't be taken for granted. America was founded on the belief that the freedom to think as you will and speak as you think are essential to democracy. Only by exercising those rights can you ensure their continued existence.

The example of a newspaper publisher who was booed off the stage of an American university sends a strong wake-up call. It's a tenet of Civics 101 that democracy needs diverse information in order to provide those who serve the citizenry with the informed consent of the governed. And a free and vigorous press is the best vehicle to fight for the whole story, not just what official Washington wants us to know. If the citizenry of the United States does not want the whole story, but only the parts of it that favor Washington's view of the war, then we shouldn't be surprised if journalists and newspaper publishers also stop asking the questions.

In time, Janis Besler Heaphy's Commencement Address may be remembered as the high mark of a public servant who, like a true patriot, showed a higher loyalty to what the country could be doing rather than what its current administration was actually doing. Heaphy may have been stung by the way some received her speech in the moment of its delivery, but in the longer run, she strengthens our values as a citizenry and the proper role of the university, which is to never stop living the questions.

The Bush Doctrine

THE WRONG ROADMAP FOR PEACE

☐ ☐ ☐

IN PRESIDENT BUSH'S COMMENCEMENT address to West Point graduates in June 2002, a speech that served, like a mind missile, as "advanced warning" of the September 2002 document, "National Security Strategy of the United States,"[104] Bush announced the overturning of a fifty-year policy of deterrence in exchange for a proactive preemptive strike policy:

> We cannot defend America and our friends by hoping for the best. We cannot put our faith in the word of tyrants, who solemnly sign non-proliferation treaties, and then systemically break them. If we wait for threats to fully materialize, we will have waited too long. Homeland defense and missile defense are part of stronger security, and they're essential priorities for America. Yet the war on terror will not be won on the defensive. We must take the battle to the enemy, disrupt his plans, and confront the worst threats before they emerge. In the world we have entered, the only path to safety is the path of action. And this nation will act...Our security will require transforming the military you will lead—a military that must be ready to strike at a moment's notice in any dark corner of the world. And our secu-

rity will require all Americans to be forward-looking and resolute, to be ready for preemptive action when necessary to defend our liberty and to defend our lives.[105]

In contrast, Kennedy in 1963 told a world shadowed by a Cold War without end: "Genuine peace must be the product of many nations, the sum of many acts. It must be dynamic, not static, changing to meet the challenge of each new generation. For peace is a process—a way of solving problems. With such a peace, there will still be quarrels and conflicting interests, as there are with families and nations. World peace, like community peace, does not require that each man love his neighbor—it requires only that they live together in mutual tolerance, submitting their disputes to a just and peaceful settlement. And history teaches us that enmities between nations, as between individuals, do not last forever. However fixed our likes and dislikes may seem, the tide of time and events will often bring surprising changes in the relations between nations and neighbors."[106]

You may wonder, as I do, how the most powerful nation on earth could so radically shift its foreign policy from one of mutuality to unilateralism. You may wonder, as I do, how a country like our own, so universally embraced in sympathy and an outpouring of global grief after September 11, 2001, could so quickly squander that goodwill and wrap its arms around a United States national security policy that seems destined to create a world not only more dangerous but also less hopeful, more depressed and less secure.

President Bush did utter more hopeful words at West Point in 2002:

We have a great opportunity to extend a just peace,

by replacing poverty, repression, and resentment around the world with hope of a better day. Through most of history, poverty was persistent, inescapable, and almost universal. In the last few decades, we've seen nations from Chile to South Korea build modern economies and freer societies, lifting millions of people out of despair and want. And there's no mystery to this achievement. The 20th century ended with a single surviving model of human progress, based on non-negotiable demands of human dignity, the rule of law, limits on the power of the state, respect for women and private property and free speech and equal justice and religious tolerance. America cannot impose this vision—yet we can support and reward governments that make the right choices for their own people. In our development aid, in our diplomatic efforts, in our international broadcasting, and in our educational assistance, the United States will promote moderation and tolerance and human rights. And we will defend the peace that makes all progress possible.

The problem with these utterances, however promising, is that the sender of the message lacks credibility. The world's eyes are focused squarely on American behavior and policies regarding the world, not blanket pronouncements of tolerance and moderation. It wasn't the United States' moderation, tolerance, and human rights that led us to begin the invasion and occupation of Iraq in March 2003. We now sit at a crossroads, where a national leader has led his country into battle to decimate a nation possessing weapons of mass destruction. Trouble is, as of October 2003, Bush hasn't been able to find any such weapons. "The sign on the White House these days might well read, 'Welcome to Credibility Gap,'" wrote David Wise in an op-ed article in *The Washington Post*.[107] And although President Bush is not the first president to lie or mislead the nation, we live in a time in which we rely on a presumption of credibility so that our government leaders can hold out any relevance in our society. If *they* are all a bunch of damn liars, then how will *we* keep the social compact between citizen and public officials?

Senator Diane Feinstein (D-CA), who voted in October 2002 in favor of granting the President authority to use force against Iraq, gave a speech on February 26, 2003, that questioned the wisdom of the Bush doctrine. She noted that that "this current strategy has little in common with candidate George W. Bush, who spoke eloquently about the need for America to conduct itself with humility in international affairs."[108] She recited Governor Bush's words from the second presidential debate between him and Vice President Gore, in which he responded to a question about America's role in the world: "If we're an arrogant nation, they'll resent us; if we're a humble nation, but strong, they'll welcome us. And our nation stands alone now in the world in terms of power, and that's why we've got to be humble, and yet project strength in a way that promotes freedom."[109]

Bush the Humble was not exactly on display as the former Texas National Guard pilot turned commander-in-chief swooped in on Navy One, landed on the deck of the battleship USS *Lincoln* and pronounced the end of major combat operations in Iraq on May 1, 2003.[110] He told the cheering soldiers:

> In these 19 months that changed the world, our actions have been focused and deliberate and proportionate to the offense. We have not forgotten the victims of September the 11th—the last phone calls,

143

the cold murder of children, the searches in the rubble. With those attacks, the terrorists and their supporters declared war on the United States. And war is what they got. Our war against terror is proceeding according to principles that I have made clear to all: Any person involved in committing or planning terrorist attacks against the American people becomes an enemy of this country, and a target of American justice. Any person, organization, or government that supports, protects, or harbors terrorists is complicit in the murder of the innocent, and equally guilty of terrorist crimes. Any outlaw regime that has ties to terrorist groups and seeks or possesses weapons of mass destruction is a grave danger to the civilized world—and will be confronted.

So much for humility. So much for lack of evidence tying Iraq to 9/11. We've got our Top Gun.

The triumphant setting for the war president was reported by the White House Office of the Press Secretary as "Remarks by the President from the USS Abraham Lincoln at Sea off the Coast of San Diego, California." The United States press representitives on deck, who were there to capture the Kodak moment, later noted that they were positioned so that no pictures could capture just how closely off shore and within clear sight of the San Diego shore the battleship was in fact moored. Like Hollywood, the event was staged and swallowed whole by a population fatigued by weeks of embeds and twenty-four-hour war. The pictures of an exuberant President Bush embraced by thousands of war-weary men and women in uniform seems destined to be used in Campaign 2004 committees to reelect the President, but even Karl Rove, the president's chief political adviser and architect of his 2004 reelection team, seems smart enough to keep the official campaign away from these potentially exploitative images of a victorious war president taking advantage of those who fought and some who died to win his reelection.

Feinstein duly noted in her speech on the Bush Doctrine that this war president is no global statesmen. "This Administration has reneged on more international treaties than any previous Administration in history including walking away from the Kyoto climate change treaty, ignoring the still unratified Comprehensive Test Ban Treaty, pulling out of negotiations on enforcement of the Biological Weapons Convention, scrapping the Anti–Ballistic Missile Treaty, and recanting the U.S. signature on the Rome Treaty to establish an International Criminal Court." Unfortunately, the United States media have done a poor job of highlighting this arrogance of American power in international relations. Most American newspapers have decreased their international news reporting in favor of home and "lifestyle sections" that are deemed more profitable to their conglomerate owners, and American broadcasters can't help but cover global issues in good guy/bad guy scenarios, making war and conflict the favored coverage. If there were only as many embedded reporters covering the international news and the United Nations on a regular basis as there were riding along with the 101 Airborne into Baghdad!

Besides the West Point commencement speech, the other precedent for the National Security Strategy Document of September 2002 was the release by the Pentagon in January 2002 of the Nuclear Posture Review (NPR), which set the stage for the Bush administration to actually consider the use of nuclear weapons in a preemptive first strike, even against nonnuclear states. The NPR presents scenarios in which the United States would not retaliate but would actually take out enemy stocks of biological and chemical weapons using a new generation of United States warheads called mininukes. The obvious environmental apocalyptic outcomes are not even discussed in these scenarios.

In September 2002, the White House released the National Security Presidential Directive, known as NSPD 17, which requires no congressional oversight or approval and which reversed in one stroke of the presidential pen a long-standing national security policy of "strategic ambiguity" regarding the United States use of nuclear weapons. The United States is the only country to ever exercise the actual use of nuclear weapons on a civilian population, and following the atomic bombing of Hiroshima and Nagasaki in August 1945, the United States government adopted the principle ambiguity coupled with the MAD promise that it would only use nuclear weapons in retaliation against the Soviet Union or other strong nuclear powers, thereby assuring mutual destruction. Together, NPR and NSPD 17 signal a possibility that the United States may consider future first-use offensive strikes using nuclear weapons. The world is alarmed, and so should the American people be alarmed, at this development. This message of possible nuclear use lowers the threshold for their use by other powers, both state and nonstate actors, including terrorist organizations and nuclear states like China, Israel, North Korea, Pakistan, and India.

As Feinstein warned, "I believe that it is critical that the United States sets a very high standard for nuclear restraint. If we do not, we may well encourage others to develop their own standards and their own nuclear arsenals. Today, both India and Pakistan are nuclear powers, and the history of bloody warfare between them presents a major and ongoing security threat to South Asia. If these countries were to follow the thinking embodied in the Administration's new nuclear policy, why would India and Pakistan not seek to integrate nuclear weapons even more into their own contingency plans—and possibly use them?"

The United States, under the leadership of Bush and his doctrine, is on the wrong path toward global peace and security. We are living in an age of the manipulation of language and thought, in which our own natural insecurities and anxieties about the economic future and possible further terrorist attacks on our homeland are being exploited by an Administration that seems destined to disengage from the world. It's as if a small group of bullies has decided to act on its own and stopped listening to anyone who disagrees with the direction they're taking. The American public is either tuning out the whole business of Washington, faithfully supporting the President and his advisers, or is too angry and immobilized to resist. And the Democratic Party has simply lost its spine, caught up in its own efforts to wrench back control from the Republicans.

We have abandoned international law and global cooperative security and replaced it with unilateralism and preemption. Do you feel more secure because of it? I don't. I have lost my faith in government to protect me because I think we are living on borrowed time and borrowed money. The federal deficit grows larger, mirrored by our own growing credibility deficit. If we continue along this path of preemption and unilateralism, we may be postponing the inevitable—a world in which the rule of law is meaningless and the King, Prince, or President with the most Might is always Right. This is not a world that operates from strength through cooperation, but from strength through vulnerability. We are replacing former anchor-store-style partner nations with convenience-store-style client and satellite states.

Picture, if you will, the brief opportunity lost when the

147

United States could have acted in close concert with our friends and allies to denounce any further violence after September 11 and used its global influence and power to build a global civilization that listens and learns and does not use force to impose its will on others. We can never capture that outpouring of global affection again, but we can change the course of our current path. The Bush administration is chartering our ship into dangerous waters. It is navigating without consulting with our traditional allies and, for the most part, without Congress, which more closely reflects the will of the people. Because of our Constitution, we have opportunities here that many of our global counterparts do not—to redress grievances, to challenge our government officials, and to vote those we can out of office if their path is the wrong one. I believe we are on the wrong path.

"If the long-term goal of our foreign policy is to help build a world where we have more allies than adversaries, more friends than enemies, and more prosperity than poverty, a doctrine of unilateral preemptive action will most certainly work against that goal." These words by the centrist Senator Diane Feinstein serve as a warning shot across our bow. The choice is ours to make to reverse course.

At the end of a video about 9/11 produced by the independent media organization Guerrilla News Network, the editors allow the viewer to ponder "the very basic choice that we have to make as a civilization. Either we will learn to bury the animosities of our ethnocentric, militant traditions, and come to understand that Earth's survival depends on our collective, unified participation, or we will sustain this cycle of violence and revenge, until humanity is returned to the status of primitivism and Earth reduced to the rubble of antiquity. It's really up to us. It really is up to us."[111]

Epilogue
WE NEED MORE PROPAGANDA, NOT LESS

□ □ □

LIKE THE COLD WAR, the Age of Terror is being fought primarily through the information war. Capture and control of the public mind is nothing to fear if we understand that propaganda is a neutral concept—any systematic process of mass persuasion—often misunderstood as censorship or lying. Most mainstream news media cover the information war like a WWF competition—in this corner, Bush rhetoric: "Ultimately, one of the best weapons, one of the truest weapons that we have against terrorism is to show the world the true strength of our character and kindness of the American people." In the other corner, Bin Laden rhetoric: "The call to wage war against America was made because America has spearheaded the crusade against the Islamic nation, sending tens of thousands of its troops to the land of the two Holy Mosques over and above its meddling in its affairs and its politics, and its support of the oppressive, corrupt and tyrannical regime that is in control."

Governments and stateless leaders have always used propaganda campaigns to wield their centralized control of message management at the expense of those who cannot. This is nothing new. The problem with focusing a spotlight on official sources of information is that we end up parsing words. What's the secret hidden message Bin Laden is sending to his cells? What will Bush say next? Our minds shut down from our own independent and critical thinking. We become caught up in the spectacle and distracted from the mundane facts. We end up as spectators, just like those fans ringside at WWF events. We tune in to CNN, MSNBC, or Fox News for the latest breaking news. Our bandwidth of context is narrowed by media companies that bring "us" to "them" through their advertising persuaders.

Let's broaden the propaganda landscape.

Did 9/11 end the deregulation and private concentration of the global media march? No, information is more centralized than ever and will continue to be squeezed into narrower channels. That's why we—the rest of us—the Chief Agitator Officers of our own e-zines and independent media centers need more propaganda, not less. We need more attempts by global citizens to arouse and educate world opinion about the real possibilities of peaceful coexistence. We need more education and organizing by citizen agitators who, like their antiglobalization activist sisters and brothers, are trying to wake up the world to the bleak consequences of power concentration.

The *New York Times* observed in an editorial on September 1, 1937, "What is truly vicious is not propaganda but a monopoly of it." At that time there was no television or Internet, instant messaging, e-mail, or cell phones. World public opinion was concerned with total control of information by government dictatorships. Today we might want to be concerned about a monopoly of official sources for news. Read a daily newspaper or watch your local news. How often do you see a private citizen quoted or interviewed? A member of a nongovernmental organization or neighborhood association? Someone not based in an elite institution of higher learning, the private sector, or government? Officialese is more prominent now than ever in the post-9/11 era.

The global elite media *are* in a difficult spot. They face challenges as to whether or not to air enemy videotapes and what information to hold back about military efforts. While decision-making is not going to get any easier for these media, citizens and consumers need to hold them accountable by *demanding* our right to hear viewpoints and perspectives from across the spectrum of public opinion. One way we can do that is by using the power that we have as media consumers and producers to build independent media coalitions. Our right to communicate is as sacred as any Pledge of Allegiance. We need to express our differences of opinion on how our governments are responding to threats and terror—and we need to educate ourselves daily with diverse, independent, in-depth, investigative news.

Right now, the war propagandists are dominating the media landscape. This should come as no surprise because war is an efficient means of carving up centralized zones of power—the power to control, the power to dominate, both through message and force.

"In a nuclear age," writes British author Philip Taylor in *Munitions of the Mind*, "we need peace propagandists, not war propagandists—people whose job it is to increase communication, understanding and dialogue between different peoples with different beliefs."[112] This is a call to arms—to arm ourselves with knowledge, content, and context generated by open and diverse channels of communication.

White House news conferences and CNN should not be watched in a vacuum, separated from the world's people. If they are, then the world belongs to the war propagandists.

What's a good counteroffensive to the propaganda environment? Every time you see something that substitutes for clear seeing and clear thinking, let the media mind managers know. Try some guerrilla marketing or culture jamming techniques along the lines of the Vancouver, B.C.–based Adbusters Foundation and magazine and send in blinders to your local TV and radio stations. Demand that the media managers start making sense and utilize all the senses, not just what will deliver eyeballs to advertisers. Join organizations that are making a difference, like Move On or Free Speech, that tap into the critical mass of progressive change in America. Read outside your comfort zone, which means that you'll have to get to know international media outlets. There are plenty online and available in your local public library.

So much of our news now seems just a brief interlude from an ad for more fantasy injections. No wonder political and civic participation is on decline. We've lost faith in public institutions altogether. Nevertheless, I have a lot of faith in the human spirit to seek out change when it looks as if nothing but conformity will do. We are amazingly creative beings and keep coming up with ways to resist becoming automatons or Stepford wives. I have the greatest faith in today's young people—they often see more clearly through the commercial clutter and are beginning to reject the mind virus that is turning our world into a global billboard.

I hope that this book helps to challenge the thinking of my global fellow citizens and empowers us all about the choices that are ours to make.

Notes

☐ ☐ ☐

Truth and Consequences

1   Howard Zinn, "Violence Doesn't Work," *The Progressive*, September 15, 2001.

2   Howard Zinn speech at Newport Harbor High, April 20, 2002.

Bermuda Mind Triangle

3   "The Propaganda War," *The Economist*, October 4, 2001.

4   See the preface of Jacques Ellul, *Propaganda* (New York: Vintage Books edition, 1973). Originally published in 1965.

5   Author interview with Konrad Kellen, March 26, 2002.

6   Alfred McClung Lee, *How to Understand Propaganda* (New York: Rinehart & Company, 1952), p. 2.

7   Victoria De Grazia, "The Selling of America, Bush Style," *New York Times*, 25 August 2002. Section 4; Page 4; Column 1; Week in Review Desk.

8   Psychological operations (psyops) is a form of information operations that packages select information in a manner to positively influence battlefield objectives. Because psyops messages are not intended to be balanced or complete, the organization's mission and bureaucracy are housed separately from those of public affairs and public diplomacy.

9   Address delivered June 17, 2002 to the Council on Foreign Relations by U.S. Rep. Henry J. Hyde (R-IL), chairman of the House International Relations Committee. In the speech entitled,

Speaking to Our Silent Allies, The Role of Public Diplomacy in U.S. Foreign Policy, Hyde urged enactment of HR 3969, the Freedom Promotion Act of 2002. Hyde released the text as a press release the same day.

"Media Collusion and the Rise of the Fourth Reich"

10 Ashleigh Banfield, Landon Lecture, Kansas State University, April 24, 2003.
11 As released in an MSNBC news statement and reported online by AlterNet, April 28, 2003.
12 See Phillip Knightly, *The First Casualty* (New York: Harcourt Brace Jovanovich), 1975, and Philip M. Taylor, *Munitions of the Mind* (Manchester: Manchester University Press), 1995.
13 Carl Bernstein, "The CIA and the Media," *Rolling Stone,* October 20, 1977, pp. 55–67.
14 Tim Weiner, "Role of CIA in Guatemala Told in Files of Publisher," *New York Times,* June 7, 1997, p. 9.
15 The official policy of the CIA includes this exception for the prohibition on employing journalists as spies or agents.
16 Martin Lee and Norman Solomon, *Unreliable Sources: A Guide to Detecting Bias in News Media* (New York: Lyle Stuart, 1990), p. 114.
17 John McArthur, *Second Front: Censorship and Propaganda in the Gulf War* (New York: Hill and Wang), 1992, p. 32.
18 "Samizdat" is a term for the secret publication and distribution of government-banned literature in the former Soviet Union, but it has also come to mean any underground or alternative, unofficial press.
19 Ben Bagdikian, *The Media Monopoly* (Boston: Beacon Press), 1997, pp. 208–210.
20 Brent Cunningham, "Re-thinking Objectivity," *Columbia Journalism Review,* July/August 2003, p. 26.
21 Ibid.

22   See James Fallows, "The Fifty-First State? The Inevitable Aftermath of Victory in Iraq," *The Atlantic Monthly*, November 2002.

23   As quoted in Cunningham, "Re-Thinking Journalism," *Columbia Journalism Review*, July/August 2003, p. 30.

In the Beginning, There Was George

24   This quote is taken from a speech by Newton Baker, Secretary of War, at a dinner given in George Creel's honor in Washington, D.C., on November 29, 1918. The speech was used as a foreword for *How We Advertised America*.

25   George Creel, *How We Advertised America* (New York: Harper & Brothers, 1920), pp. 4–5.

26   Ibid.

27   As Creel expressed it, "While America's summons was answered without question by the citizenship as a whole, it is to be remembered that during the three and a half years of our neutrality the land had been torn by a thousand divisive prejudices, stunned by the voices of anger and confusion, and muddled by the pull and haul of opposed interests."

28   Ibid., p. 5.

29   Ibid., p. 7.

30   Donald Rumsfeld, "A New Kind of War," *New York Times*, September 27, 2001.

31   "Foreign Media Reaction Report," U.S. Department of State, October 2001.

32   For a fuller analysis of the debate over America's losing the propaganda war, see John Lumpkin, "Truth Becomes a Casualty in Afghan War," *Associated Press*, October 27, 2001; "Imagery first, weaponry second: propaganda war," *National Journal*, November 3, 2001; and "Who's Winning the Propaganda War?," ABC News' Nightline with Ted Koppel, October 18, 2001.

33   Kathy Hoffman, "Former Ambassador Says U.S. Doing Poor Job Explaining its Side," *Associated Press*, October 25, 2001.

34   Elizabeth Becker, "In the War on Terrorism, a Battle to Shape Public Opinion," *New York Times*, November 11, 2001, A1.

35   See author comments in Vinay Menon's article, "Tinseltown continues its long tradition of backing Washington in wartime— but how far should it go?" in the *Toronto Star*, October 28, 2001. Also see Howard Rosenberg, "Propaganda Machine Signs Enlistees," *Los Angeles Times*, November 12, 2001, F10.

36   For a discussion of U.S. reluctance to use the word "propaganda," see the revised and expanded second edition of *Propaganda, Inc.: Selling America's Culture to the World* (New York: Seven Stories Press, 2002).

37   Two monumental press leaks were public relations disasters for the Bush administration: The *Los Angeles Times'* William Arkin leaked a report of the administration's post-9/11 document, Nuclear Posture Review (NPR), that made a case for limited nuclear strikes against "axis of evil" countries, and the *New York Times* carried a front-page story on February 19, 2002 about the Pentagon's Office of Strategic Influence.

38   See the website for AVOT at www.avot.org and read the ACTA report, "Defending Civilization: How Our Universities are Failing and What Can Be Done About It," at www.goacta.org.

When Harry Met George

39   President Harry S Truman.

40   President George W. Bush.

41   It is worth noting that the rise of the "persuader-in-chief" function over the last 100 years. Woodrow Wilson had George Creel, whose Creel Committee ran propaganda operations for the President in World War I. Harry S. Truman had George Elsey, said to be very interested in international persuasion and psywar efforts. Dwight Eisenhower had his official propagandist, C. D. Jackson, as documented in Blanche Wiesen Cook's *The Declassified Eisenhower*. The *New York Times* reported on November 11, 2001, that the White House was waging "what may be the most ambitious wartime communications effort

since World War II." President Bush's chief domestic persuader was Karen Hughes, the White House communications director, who announced her departure from the White House in April 2002. She cited the need to spend more time with family and a feeling of homesickness for Texas as main reasons for the Washington departure but assured reporters that she would continue to advise the President from her home in Texas.

42   Edward Barrett, *Truth is Our Weapon* (New York: Funk & Wagnalls Company), p. 73.

43   President Harry S Truman, psychological offensive (psyop) speech before the American Society of Newspaper Editors, Washington, D.C., April 20, 1950.

44   The NSC-68 Policy Document includes a section called "U.S. Intentions and Capabilities—Actual and Potential," that lays out the overall United States policy that still defines American power in the twenty-first century. It "rejects the concept of isolation and affirms the necessity of our positive participation in the world community." One of the most important signals of American strength is identified as a superior military and the maintenance of a strong military posture to "contain" Soviet aggression. In the political and psychological fields, "The vast majority of Americans are confident that the system of values which animates our society—the principles of freedom, tolerance, the importance of the individual, and the supremacy of reason over will—are valid and more vital than the ideology which is the fuel of Soviet dynamism. Translated into terms relevant to the lives of other peoples—our system of values can become perhaps a powerful appeal to millions who now seek or find in authoritarianism a refuge from anxieties, bafflement, and insecurity...These capabilities within us constitute a great potential force in our international relations. The potential within us of bearing witness to the values by which we live holds promise for a dynamic manifestation to the rest of the world of the vitality of our system. The essential tolerance of our world outlook, our generous and constructive impulses, and

the absence of covetousness in our international relations are assets of potentially enormous influence."

45   Rep. Henry Hyde, Chairman, House International Relations Subcommittee, News Advisory, October 9, 2001.

46   Rep. Ed Royce, "The Taliban and the terrorists they are harboring use propaganda and censorship to maintain power. They must be countered." Press release, November 7, 2001.

47   Alfred McClung Lee, *How to Understand Propaganda* (New York: Rinehart & Company, Inc., 1952).

48   Since the Cold War era, American dissent is cast with suspicion, as measured in the following statement from NSC-68: "The very virtues of our system likewise handicap us in certain respects in our relations with our allies. *While it is a general source of strength to us that our relations with our allies are conducted on a basis of persuasion and consent rather than compulsion and capitulation, it is also evident that dissent among us can become a vulnerability.* Sometimes the dissent has its principal roots abroad in situations about which we can do nothing. Sometimes it arises largely out of certain weaknesses within ourselves, about which we can do something—our native impetuosity and a tendency to expect too much from people widely divergent from us."

49   Martin Luther King, Jr., Riverside Church, April 4, 1967.

50   Walter Lippmann, *The Phantom Public* (New York: Macmillan Company, 1927).

Why I Write vs. Why We Fight

51   Joseph McBride, *Frank Capra: The Catastrophe of Success*. New York: Simon and Schuster, 1992, p. 455.

52   William Bennett, *Why We Fight: Moral Clarity and the War on Terrorism*. New York: Doubleday, 2002, p. 39.

53   Ibid., p. 40.

Opinion Control

54   See also, Herbert I. Schiller, "Manipulating Hearts and Minds,"in *Triumph of the Image: The Media's War in the*

Persian Gulf, Hamid Mowlana, George Gerbner, and Herbert I. Schiller (Eds.), Westview Press, 1992, pp. 22–29.

55 Tom Wicker, "An Unknown Casualty," *New York Times*, March 20, 1991, p. A17.

56 As quoted in Schiller, "Manipulating Hearts and Minds," p. 23.

57 *Columbia Journalism Review*, March–April 1991, pp. 25–28.

58 Bob Sipschen, "The Media Rewrite, Review the Gulf War," *Los Angeles Times*, March 7, 1991, p. E2.

59 As quoted in the *New York Times*, March 23, 1991, p. A4.

60 As reported in the *Los Angeles Times*, March 25, 1991, p. A9.

61 Ibid., p. E1.

62 Eric Lichtblau, "U.S. Uses Terror Law to Pursue Crimes From Drugs to Swindling," *New York Times*, September 28, 2003, p. A!.

63 George W. Bush, Graduation Speech at West Point, June 1, 2002.

64 Nicholas Lemann, "The War on What?: The White House and the Debate about whom to fight next," *The New Yorker*, September 9, 2002.

65 George Orwell, "Politics and the English Language," 1946.

66 George W. Bush, Radio Address by the President to the Nation, October 12, 2002.

67 Stephen O'Leary, "The Anti-War Movement on the Web," *Online Journalism Review*, October 18, 2002.

68 Bob Woodward, CNN's *Larry King Live*, November 18, 2002.

69 Jacques Ellul, *Propaganda*. (New York: Vintage Books), 1973.

70 William Odom, C-SPAN's *Washington Journal*, November 24, 2002.

71 "Brand-builder's elegant task, *Financial Times* (London), April 19, 1999.

72 Secretary of State Colin L. Powell, "Function 150 of the President's Budget for Fiscal Year 2002," Testimony before the House Budget Committee, March 15, 2001.

73 Charlotte Beers, Senate Confirmation Hearings, October 2, 2001.

74 Peter Carlson, "The U.S.A. Account; Ad Woman Charlotte Beer's New Campaign: Getting the World to Buy America, The *Washington Post*, Style section, p. C1.

75 Andrew Alexander, Daily Mail, October 2001.

76 Quoted in Rance Crain, "Selling idea of freedom is most important assignment for Beers. *Advertising Age*, Nov 5, 2001 v72 p12.

77 Steve Lopez, "We Need People, Not Propaganda, to Sell America to the World," *Los Angeles Times*, October 29, 2001, p. B1.

78 Senator J. William Fulbright, *The Arrogance of Power* (New York: Vintage Books, 1965), p. 27.

79 See "Charlotte Beers; How World's Top Woman Ad Executive Hit the Heights," *Los Angeles Times*, AP Wire, May 4, 1992, p. D6.

80 Interview transcript, *Good Morning America*, December 14, 2001, Burrelle's Information Services, ABC News.

81 Rewards for Justice (www.rewardsforjustice.net)

82 Johanna Neuman, "State Department Ad Campaign Asks Public to Catch Terrorists," December 14, 2001, Los Angeles Times.

83 State Department Briefing on the Rewards for Justice Program, Secretary of State Colin L. Powell, Under Secretary Charlotte Beers, and Assistant Secretary David G. Carpenter, December 13, 2001, Washington, D.C.

84 Alexandra Starr, "Building Brand America," *Business Week*, December 10, 2001.

85 Marci MacDonald, "Branding America," *U.S. News & World Report*, November 26, 2001, p. 46.

86 Michele Kelemen, NPR's *Weekend All Things Considered*, December 15, 2001.

87 Michael Schudson, *Advertising: The Uneasy Persuasion* (New York: Basic Books), p. 215.

88 Ad Council Campaign for Freedom, located online at http://www.adcouncil.org/campaigns/campaign_for_freedom/

89 See Karen Lowry Miller, "U.S. Brands Losing Affection Overseas," in *Newsweek*, July 20, 2003.

90 Thomas C. Sorensen, *The Word War: The Story of American Propaganda* (New York: Harper & Row), 1968, p. 145.

91 Garth S. Jowett and Victoria O'Donnell, *Propaganda and Persuasion* (Thousand Oaks, CA: Sage), p. 149.

92   Vanessa O'Connell, "Marketing and Advertising: U.S. Suspends TV Ad Campaign Aimed at Winning Over Muslims, *Wall Street Journal*, January 16, 2003.

The Myth of the Lone Dissenter

93   See the State Department website, Common Ground, at www.opendialogue.org

94   See Alfred McClung Lee and Elizabeth Briant Lee, *The Fine Art of Propaganda*, Institute for Propaganda Analysis (New York: Harcourt, Brace and Company), 1939.

95   Herbert Romerstein, "Who is Barbara Lee?" *Washington Times*, September 18, 2001, p. A16.

96   See "10 days in September," The Washington Post's eight-part series on the war's beginnings, told to Bob Woodward from the White House perspective.

97   Feral Keane, "Public Enemy Number One?," The London *Independent*, February 4, 2003, p. 4.

98   Rob Morse, "Barbara Lee and Rush Limbaugh Eye to Eye at Last," *San Francisco Chronicle*, August 16, 2002, p. A2.

Uncle Sam and the "Arab Street"

99   Andrea Koppel, "CNN Showdown: Iraq," March 27, 2003.

100 BBC News Web site, October 10, 2003, http://news.bbc.co.uk/2/hi/americas/3179606.stm

101 For reference, see Thomas L Friedman, "Memo to: The Arab Street," *New York Times*, January 12, 2000.

102 Well over half the populations of Egypt, Syria, Saudi Arabia, Iran, and Iraq are under twenty-five years old, according to the International Programs Center at the Census Bureau. In Pakistan, the number is 61 percent; in Afghanistan, 62 percent. Reported by Elaine Sciolino, "Radicalism: Is the Devil in the Demographics?" *New York Times*, December 9, 2001.

103 The Fulbright program was born in the aftermath of World War II and has allowed over 100,000 Americans to study, teach, and conduct research abroad. The Fulbright Program currently oper-

ates in 140 countries. Approximately 150,000 students and scholars from countries throughout the world have studied in the United States.

The Bush Doctrine

104 Read the entire 35-page document online at http://www.white-house.gov/nsc/nss.html

105 George W. Bush, Commencement Address at the United States Military Academy, West Point, June 1, 2002.

106 John F. Kennedy, speech at American University, June 10, 1963.

107 David Wise, "If Bush is Lying, He's Not the First," *Washington Post*, Page B01, June 15, 2003.

108 Diane Feinstein, "The New Bush Doctrine: The Wrong Path to Our Nation's Security?" Speech before The Center for National Policy, Washington, D.C., February 26, 2003.

109 George W. Bush, General Election Presidential Debate, Wake Forest University, North Carolina, October 11, 2000.

110 George W. Bush, "President Bush Announces Combat Operations in Iraq Have Ended," The White House. http://www.whitehouse.gov/news/releases/2003/05/iraq/200305 01-15.html

111 Guerrilla News Network, "S-11: Channel Surfing the Apocalypse," October 2001.

Epilogue

112 Taylor, Philip. *Munitions of the Mind: A History of Propaganda From the Ancient World to the Present Day* (New York and Manchester, Manchester University Press, 1995.) p. 303.

Index

About the Author

☐☐☐

NANCY SNOW is assistant professor in the College of Communications at California State University, Fullerton, and adjunct assistant professor in the Annenberg School for Communication, University of Southern California. Since 9/11, Snow has become a frequent media commentator and public speaker on American foreign policy, influence, persuasion, propaganda, and the root causes of anti-Americanism. She received her Ph.D. in international relations from the School of International Service at The American University in Washington, D.C. From 1992 to 1994, she worked as a cultural affairs specialist and Fulbright program desk officer at the United States Information Agency and as intergovernmental liaison in the Bureau of Refugee Programs, U.S. State Department. She was a Fulbright scholar to Germany and a German Academic Exchange Service (DAAD) fellow at the University of California, Berkeley. Snow is also the author of *Propaganda, Inc.: Selling American's Culture to the World*, in addition to many published articles in professional and mainstream publications including the *Los Angeles Times* and *Newsday*. She can be reached online at www.NancySnow.com.

An American journalist, GREG PALAST reports for BBC Television's *Newsnight,* and is author of the bestseller *The Best Democracy Money Can Buy: An Investigative Reporter Reveals the Truth About Globalization, Corporate Cons and High-Finance Fraudsters* (Penguin Plume 2003).

OTHER OPEN MEDIA TITLES

DEAD HEAT: GLOBAL JUSTICE AND GLOBAL WARMING
Tom Athanasiou and Paul Baer
$9.95 / ISBN:1-58322-491-2

SILENCING POLITICAL DISSENT: HOW POST-SEPT. 11 ANTI-
TERRORISM MEASURES THREATEN OUR CIVIL LIBERTIES
Nancy Chang
Foreword by Howard Zinn
$9.95 / ISBN: 1-58322-493-9

9-11
Noam Chomksy
$8.95 / ISBN: 1-58322-489-0

MEDIA CONTROL: THE SPECTACULAR
ACHIEVEMENTS OF PROPAGANDA
Noam Chomsky
$8.95 / ISBN: 1-58322-536-6

ARE PRISONS OBSOLETE?
Angela Y. Davis
$8.95 / ISBN: 1-58322-581-1

GLOBAL GOVERNANCE: THE BATTLE OVER
PLANETARY POWER
Kristin Dawkins
$9.95 / ISBN: 1-58322-580-3

EXORCISING TERROR: THE INCREDIBLE UNENDING TRIAL OF GEN-
ERAL AUGUSTO PINOCHET
Ariel Dorfman
$11.95 / ISBN: 1-58322542-0

NORTH KOREA/SOUTH KOREA
John Feffer
$9.95 / ISBN: 1-58322-603-6

FULL SPECTRUM DOMINANCE
Rahul Mahajan
$9.95 / ISBN: 1-58322-578-1

OUR MEDIA, NOT THEIRS: THE DEMOCRATIC STRUGGLE
AGAINST CORPORATE MEDIA
Robert W. McChesney & John Nichols
$9.95 / ISBN:1-58322-549-8

COLOMBIA AND THE UNITED STATES
Mario A. Murillo
$9.95 / ISBN: 1-58322-606-0

THE PROJECT CENSORED GUIDE TO INDEPENDENT MEDIA
AND ACTIVISM
Project Censored
$10.95 / ISBN: 1-58322-468-8

ISRAEL/PALESTINE: HOW TO END THE WAR OF 1948
Tanya Reinhart
$11.95 / ISBN:1-58322-538-2

NEGATIVE ETHNICITY:
FROM BIAS TO GENOCIDE
Koigi wa Wamwere
$10.95 / ISBN: 1-58322-576-5

TERRORISM AND WAR
Howard Zinn
$9.95 / ISBN: 1-58322-493-9

ARTISTS IN TIMES OF WAR
Howard Zinn
$9.95 / ISBN: 1-58322-602-8

More Info: www.sevenstories.com / To order call: 800. 596 7437